A Funny Thing Happened on the Way to the Health Fair©

Complied and Edited by Fred Neil

"A Funny Thing Happened on the Way to the Health Fair," compiled and edited by Fred Neil. ISBN 1-58939-212-4 (softcover).

Library of Congress Control Number: 2002107753.

Published 2002 by Virtualbookworm. com Publishing Inc. , P. O. Box 9949, College Station, TX , 77842, US.

Printed in the United States of America.

AUTHOR'S NOTE

This book is so funny, it will heal the stitches it keeps you in!

This book is 73.5% F Rated (for Family) and 26.5% R-17 (If you haven't told your kids about the Birds and the Bees by the age of 17, shame on you!)

This book is dedicated to my father!

As a small boy, my father, a pharmacist, said to me, "Son, you did not choose to be on this earth, but you are here. It is a very tough place to live with lots of stinkers around to make life miserable. You have a choice. You can add to the misery, or you can make life more enjoyable."

Dad, this is my tribute to you!

Acknowledgements

Very special thanks to my wife whom I subject to continual "Pun"ishment against the "Quip"ing Post.

Deep appreciation is also expressed to contributors Manny Krinetz, Mo Dutterer, Lynn Divirgilio, and particularly Larry Reba (aka Manny, Mo, Larry, and Lynn), and to all of those anonymous story spinners who cared enough share the laughter.

Preface

Laughs are a serious business when it comes to health. I remember hearing that the phrase, "Laughter is the Best Medicine" came from the pen of the late, brilliant editor of the Saturday Review, Norman Cousins. Cousins had battled through a life-threatening illness and learned that laughter was a key to his survival. He watched old Marx Brothers Movies. A prolific author, Mr. Cousins wrote a number of books dealing the state of the mind vis a vis illness.

In this modern world, a ride on the Internet reveals web sites and books dedicated to laughter as medicine.

In February 2002, the annual conference of the Association for Applied and Therapeutic Humor, founded in 1988, met in Baltimore. The participants shared experiences of how humor helps even during the most horrific times such as holocaust, personal tragedies, natural disasters, and the terrorists attacks at the World Trade Center twin towers on September 11, 2001.

However, the idea that laughter has medicinal benefits has a long history. As recently as March 2002, at the Gridiron Club "bash the brass" annual laffathon event in Washington, D.C., President Abraham Lincoln's remarks on the subject were recalled. As quoted in the Washington Post on March 11, 2002, United States Senate Majority Leader Tom Daschle reported, "'With the fearful strain upon me day and night,' Lincoln had told his stricken Cabinet, 'If I did not laugh, I should die. You need this medicine as much as I do.'"

Just as chicken soup has proved beneficial when you have a cold, " A Funny Thing Happened on the Way to the Health Fair" is chicken soup for your mind. I am not advocating tossing away your prescriptions or stop seeing your doctor, just use this book frequently as adjunct care.
Better still, read two stories and tell them to a friend in next morning.

In the words of a genius, whose name escapes me, "It couldn't hurt!"

Table of Contents

Section One: The Bible Revisited

Just look around you if you don't believe God had a sense of humor!

The Lord Giveth
In the beginning...

The Lord created Adam. After a while Adam became unhappy and prayed to the Lord for help.

The Lord asked him, "What is wrong?"

Adam said, "I don't have anyone to talk to."

The Lord said "I will make you a companion. I will call her woman. She will gather food for you, cook for you, and when you discover clothing she'll wash it for you. She will always agree with every decision you make. She will not nag you and will always be the first to admit she was wrong when you've had a disagreement."

Adam asked The Lord, "What will a woman like this cost?"

The Lord paused then replied, "An arm and a leg."

Then Adam asked, "What can I get for a rib?"

The rest is history.

One day The Lord spoke to Adam...

"I've got some good news and some bad news."

Adam said "Oh, Lord, please let me hear good news first."

The Lord explained, "I've given you two new organs. One is called a brain. It will allow you to create new things, solve problems, and have intelligent conversations with Eve.

"The other organ I give you is called a penis. It will give you and Eve great physical pleasure and enable you to reproduce an intelligent life form called children who will grow and populate this planet. Eve will be very, very happy that you now have this organ."

Adam, very excited, exclaimed, "These are great gifts you have given to me. What could possibly be bad news after such great tidings?"

The Lord said with great sorrow,"You will never be able to use these two gifts at the same time."

The Origin of Pets

A newly discovered chapter in the Book of Genesis has provided the answer to "Where do pets come from?"

Adam and Eve said, "Lord, when we were in the garden, you walked with us every day. Now we do not see you any more. We are lonesome here, and it is difficult for us to remember how much you love us."

And God said, "No problem! I will create a companion for you that will be with you forever and who will be a reflection of my love for you, so that you will love me even when you cannot see me. Regardless of how selfish or childish or unlovable you may be, this new companion will accept you as you are and will love you as I do, in spite of yourselves."

And God created a new animal to be a companion for Adam and Eve. And it was a good animal.

And God was pleased.

And the new animal was pleased to be with Adam and Eve and he wagged his tail.

And Adam said, "Lord, I have already named all the animals in the Kingdom and I cannot think of a name for this new animal."

And God said, "No problem. Because I have created this new animal to be a reflection of my love for you, his name will be a reflection of my own name, and you will call him DOG."

And Dog lived with Adam and Eve and was a companion to them and loved them.

And they were comforted.

And God was pleased.

And Dog was content and wagged his tail.

After a while, it came to pass that an angel came to the Lord and said, "Lord, Adam and Eve have become filled with pride. They strut and preen like peacocks and they believe they are worthy of adoration. Dog has indeed taught them that they are loved, but perhaps too well."

And God said, "No problem! I will create for them a companion who will be with them forever and who will see them as they are. The companion will remind them of their limitations, so they will know that they are not always worthy of adoration."

And God created CAT to be a companion to Adam and Eve.

And Cat would not obey them. And when Adam and Eve gazed into Cat's eyes, they were reminded that they were not the supreme beings.

And Adam and Eve learned humility.
And they were greatly improved.

And God was pleased.

And Dog was happy.

And Cat didn't give a damn one way or the other.

And Then The Lord Created....

On the very first day, The Lord created the cow. He said to the cow. "Today, I have created you! As a cow, you must go to the field with the farmer all day long. You will work all day
under the sun! I will give you a life span of 50 years."

The cow objected. "What? This tough life you want me to live for 50 years? Let me have 20 years. The other 30 years - I'll give back to you." The Lord agreed.

On the second day, The Lord created the dog. The Lord said to the dog, " What you are supposed to do is to sit all day by the door of your house. Any people that come by, or in, you will
bark at them! I'll give you a life span of 20 years!"

The dog objected. "What? All day long I have to sit by the door? No way! Let me live for only ten years. I give you back my other 10 years of life!" The Lord agreed.

On the third day, The Lord created the monkey. He said to the monkey, "A monkey has to entertain people. You've got to make them laugh and do monkey tricks. And I'll give you a 20 year life span."

The monkey objected. "What? Make them laugh? Do monkey faces and tricks? Ten years will do, and the other 10 years I give back to you." The Lord agreed.

On the fourth day, The Lord created man and said to him, "Your job is to sleep, eat, and play. You will enjoy very much in your life. All you need to do is to enjoy and do nothing. For this kind of life, I'll give you a 20 year life span."

The man objected. "What? Such a good life! Eat, play, sleep, do nothing? Enjoy the best and you expect me to live only for 20 years? No way, Lord! Why don't we make a deal?

Since cow gave you back 30 years, dog gave you back 10 years, and monkey gave you back 10 years, I will take them from you! That makes my life span 70 years, right?" And The Lord agreed.

And That Is Why...
In our first 20 years, we eat, sleep, play, enjoy the best and do nothing much.

For the next 30 years, we work all day long, suffer and get to support the family.

For the next 10 years, we entertain our grandchildren by making monkey faces and doing monkey tricks.

And for the last 10 years, we stay at home, sit in front of the door and bark at people.

Another View....

One day in the Garden of Eden, Eve calls out to God ..."Lord, I have a problem!"

What's the problem Eve?

"Lord, I know you've created me and have provided this beautiful garden and all of these wonderful animals, and that hilarious comedic snake, but I'm just not happy.

"Why is that Eve?," came the reply from above.

"Lord, I am lonely. And I'm sick to death of apples."

"Well, Eve, in that case, I have a solution. I shall create a man for you."

"What's a 'man,' Lord?"

"This 'man' will be a flawed creature, with many bad traits. He'll lie, cheat, and be vainglorious; all in all, he'll give you a hard time. But, he'll be bigger, faster, and will like to hunt and kill things. I'll create him in such a way that he will satisfy your physical needs. He'll be witless and will revel in childish things like fighting and kicking a ball about. He won't be too smart, so he'll also need your advice to think properly.

"Sounds great," says Eve, with an ironically raised eyebrow. "What's the catch, Lord?"

"As I said, he'll be proud, arrogant, and self-admiring, so you'll have to let him believe that I made him first ...so, just remember...it's our secret ... woman-to-woman!"

The Eleventh Commandment

The Lord called to Moses to come before him.

"Yes, Lord."

"Moses, I plan to send you back to earth and back in time."

"But why, Lord?"

"I am very disturbed by what I see happening on earth and particularly in America, one of my favorite nations."

"What disturbs you Lord?"

"Men in high places... leaders... elected officials, are taking advantage of young, vulnerable women. These men should know better. They have to know that I'm watching."

"What do you plan do, Lord?"

"I'm going to give them a warning!"

"How do you plan to do that, Lord?"

"I plan to send you back to earth to the time I guided you to write the 10 commandments... and I will have you write the 11th commandment."

"What shall I write as the 11th commandment, Lord?"

"Thou shalt not comfort thy Rod with thy Staff."

De Je Vue

Airforce One landed at Ben Gurian airport in Israel. President George W. Bush, en route to a peace conference, saw an old man with white hair, a long white beard, wearing a long white robe and holding a staff. He walked up to the man, who was staring at the ceiling, and said, "Excuse me sir, aren't you Moses?" The man stood perfectly still and continued to stare at the ceiling, saying nothing.

President Bush, turned to his entourage, and shrugged. George W asked, a little louder this time, "Excuse me sir, aren't you Moses?"

Again the old man stared at the ceiling motionless without saying a word.

George W tried a third time, louder yet. "Please, I am here to try to bring peace to the Middle-East. Please won't you answer me? Are you Moses?"

Again, no movement or words from the old man. He continued to stare at the ceiling.

George W's signaled to one of his aides and asked him "Do you think this man is deaf or extremely rude?. I have asked him three times if he was Moses, and he has not answered."

To which the man, still staring at the ceiling finally replied, "I can hear you, and, yes, I am Moses... but the last time I spoke to a bush, I spent 40 years wandering in the wilderness."

In Cleveland, The Lord spoke on billboards...

Let's meet at my house Sunday before the game.
-God

C'mon over and bring the kids.
-God

What part of "Thou Shalt Not..." didn't you understand?
-God

We need to talk.
-God

Keep using my name in vain, I'll make rush hour longer.
-God

Loved the wedding, invite me to the marriage.
-God

That "Love Thy Neighbor" thing... I meant it.
-God

I love you and you and you and you and...
-God

Will the road you're on get you to my place?
-God

Follow me.
-God

Big bang theory? You've got to be kidding!
-God

My way is the high way.
-God

Need directions?
-God

You think it's hot here?
-God

Have you read my #1 best seller? There will be a test.
-God

Do you have any idea where you're going?
-God

I don't question your existence so don't question mine.
- God

Don't make me come down there.
-God

A Lesson from the Bible

A man has been in business for many, many years and the business is going down the drain. He is seriously contemplating suicide and he doesn't know what to do. He goes to his Minister to seek his advice. He tells the Minister about all of his problems in the business and asks what he should do.

The Minister says, "Take a beach chair and a Bible and put them in your car and take them down to the ocean. Go to the water's edge. Take the beach chair out of the car, sit on it and take the bible out and open it up. The wind will riffle the pages for a while and eventually the Bible will stay open at a particular page. Read the first words your eyes fall on and those words will tell you what to do."

The man does as he is told. He places a beach chair and a Bible in his car and drives down to the beach. He sits on the chair at the water's edge and opens the Bible. The wind riffles the pages and stops at a particular page. He looks down at the Bible and his eyes fall on words that tell him what he should do.

A year later the man and his family come back to see the Minister. The man is wearing a $1,000 Italian suit, The wife is decked out with a full-length mink coat and the child is dressed in beautiful silk.

The man hands the Minister a thick envelope full of money and tells him that he wants to donate this money to the church in order to thank the Minister for his wonderful advice. The Minister is delighted. He asks the man what words in the Bible brought this good fortune to him.

The man replies, "Chapter 11."

Not Exactly Biblical

One day while walking down the street a highly successful Human Resources Director was tragically hit by a bus and she died. Her soul arrived up in heaven where she was met at the Pearly Gates by St. Peter himself.

"Welcome to Heaven," said St. Peter. "Before you get settled in, though, it seems we have a problem. You see, strangely enough, we've never once had a Human Resources Director make it this far and we're not really sure what to do with you."

"No problem, just let me in" said the woman.

"Well, I'd like to, but I have higher orders. What we're going to do is let you have a day in Hell and a day in Heaven and then you can choose whichever one you want to spend an eternity in."

"Actually, I think I've made up my mind, I prefer to stay in Heaven," said the woman.

"Sorry, we have rules..." And with that St. Peter put the woman in an elevator and it went down-down-down to hell.

The doors opened and she found herself stepping out onto the putting green of a beautiful golf course. In the distance was a country club and standing in front of her were all her friends - fellow executives that she had worked with. They were all dressed in fashion designer clothes and they cheering when they saw her. They ran up and kissed her on both cheeks and they talked about old times. Then, they played a splendid round of golf using the finest golf clubs available that were fitted for her. At night, they went to the country club where she enjoyed the best steak and lobster dinner she had ever eaten. She met the Devil who was actually a really nice guy (kinda cute) and she had a great time telling jokes and dancing. She was having such a good time that before she knew it, it was time to leave. Everybody shook her hand and waved good-bye as she got on the elevator.

The elevator went up-up-up and opened back up at the Pearly Gates. St. Peter was waiting for her.

"Now it's time to spend a day in heaven," he said. She spent the next 24 hours lounging around on clouds and playing the harp and singing. She had a great time and before she knew it her 24 hours were up and St. Peter came and got her. "You've spent a day in hell and you've spent a day in heaven. Now you must choose your eternity," he said. The woman paused for a second and then replied, "Well, I never thought I'd say this, I mean, Heaven has been really great and all, but I think I had a better time in Hell."

St. Peter escorted her to the elevator and again she went down-down-down to Hell.

When the doors of the elevator opened she found herself standing in a desolate wasteland covered in garbage and filth. She saw her friends were dressed in rags and were picking up the garbage and putting it in sacks. The Devil came up to her and put his arm around her. "I don't understand," stammered the woman, "yesterday I was here and there was a golf course and a country club and we ate lobster and we danced and had a great time. Now, all there is a wasteland of garbage and all my friends look miserable. "

The Devil looked at her and smiled. "Yesterday, we were recruiting you. Today, you're staff ......"

Holy Golf?

Shortly after the Pope had apologized to the Nation of Israel for the treatment of Jews by the Catholic Church over the years, Ehud Barak, who was then the leader of Israel, sent back a message to the Pope. The proposal was for a friendly game of golf to be played between the two leaders or their representatives to show the friendship and ecumenical spirit shared by the Catholic and Jewish faiths. The Pope met with his College of Cardinals to discuss the proposal.

"Your Holiness," said one of the Cardinals, "Mr. Barak wants to challenge you to a game of golf to show that you are old and unable to compete I am afraid that this would tarnish our image to the world."

The Pope thought about this and as he had never held a golf club in his life asked, "Don't we have a Cardinal to represent me?"

"None that plays golf very well," a Cardinal replied. "But," he added, "there is a man named Jack Nicklaus, an American golfer who is a devout Catholic. We can offer to make him a Cardinal, and ask him to play Mr. Barak as your personal representative. In addition to showing our spirit of cooperation, we'll also win the match."

Everyone agreed it was a great idea. The call was made. Nicklaus was honored and agreed to play as a representative of the Pope.

The day after the match, Nicklaus reported to the Vatican to inform the Pope of the result. "I have some good news and some bad news, Your Holiness," said the golfer.

"Tell me the good news, Cardinal Nicklaus," said the Pope.

"Well, Your Holiness, I don't like to brag, but even though I've played some pretty terrific rounds of golf in my life, this was the best I have ever played, by far. I must have been inspired from above. My drives were long and true, my irons were accurate and purposeful, and my putting was perfect. With all due respect, my play was truly miraculous."

"How can there be bad news?" the Pope asked.

Nicklaus sighed, "I lost to Rabbi Tiger Woods by three strokes."

Section Two: Travel Along Unbeaten Paths

Travel is enlightening... and damn funny too!

Way Out West

An attractive woman from New York was driving through a remote part of New Mexico when her car broke down. A Native American on horseback came along and offered her a ride to a nearby town. She climbed up behind him on the horse and they rode off.

The ride was uneventful except that every few minutes the Native American would let out a whoop so loud that it would echo from the surrounding hills.

When they arrived in town, he let her off at the local service station, yelled one final, "Yahoo!" and rode off.

"What did you do to get that Indian so excited?" asked the service station attendant.

"Nothing. I merely sat behind him on the horse, put my arms around his waist, and held onto his saddle horn so I wouldn't fall off."

"Lady," the attendant said, "Indians ride bareback."

Tower Talk

During taxi, the crew of a US AIR departure flight to Ft. Lauderdale made a wrong turn and came nose to nose with a United 727. The irate ground controller (a female) screamed, "US Air 2771, where are you going? I told you to turn right on "Charlie" taxiway; you turned right on "Delta. Stop right there! I know it's difficult to tell the difference between C's & D's, but get it right!"

Continuing her lashing to the embarrassed crew, she was now shouting hysterically, "God, you've screwed everything up; it'll take forever to sort this out. You stay right there and don't
move until I tell you to! Then, I want you to go exactly where I tell you, when I tell you, and how I tell you. You got that, US Air 2771?"

The humbled pilot responded, "Yes, Ma'am." The ground control frequency went terribly silent; no one wanted to engage the irate ground controller in her current state. Tension in every cockpit at the airport was running high.

Then an unknown male pilot broke the silence and asked, "Wasn't I married to you once?"

OOPS

One thing leads to another...

The jetliner was taking off from O'Hare. Shortly after it reached the cruising altitude, the captain began his normal welcoming remarks...

"Ladies and gentlemen, this is your captain speaking. . . Welcome to Flight 4295, nonstop from Chicago to Newark. Our weather ahead is good and we have a tail wind. We anticipate a smooth and uneventful flight. So sit back and relax - OH NO! WHAT HAVE YOU DONE?!"

Silence followed and after a few minutes, the intercom came to life once again. The calm voice of the captain said, "Ladies and Gentlemen, I am so sorry if I scared you earlier, but while I was finishing my announcement, the flight-attendant brought me a cup of coffee and spilled the whole thing right my lap. You should see the front of my pants!"

A passenger in Coach said, "Yeah, right... He should see the back of mine!"

The Love Boat

A young woman was so depressed that she decided to end her life by throwing herself into the ocean. She went down to the docks and was about to leap into the frigid water when a handsome young sailor saw her tottering on the edge of the pier crying.

He took pity on her and said, "Look, you've got a lot to live for. I'm off to Europe in the morning, and if you like, I can stow you away on my ship. I'll take good care of you and bring you food every day."

Moving closer he slipped his arm round her shoulder and added, "I'll keep you happy, and you'll keep me happy."

The girl nodded yes. After all, what did she have to lose?

That night, the sailor brought her aboard and hid her in a lifeboat. From then on every night he brought her sandwiches and a piece of fruit, and they made passionate love until dawn.

Three weeks later, during a routine inspection, she was discovered by the Captain.

"What are you doing here?" the Captain asked.

"I have an arrangement with one of the sailors," she explained. "I get food and this trip to Europe, and he's screwing me."

"He sure is, lady," the Captain said. "This is the Staten Island Ferry."

Into the Air, Junior Bird People

Occasionally, airline attendants make an effort to make the "in-flight safety lecture" and their other announcements a bit more entertaining. Here are some real examples that have been heard or reported:

From a Southwest Airlines employee: "There may be 50 ways to leave your lover, but there are only 4 ways out of this airplane."

Pilot: "Folks, we have reached our cruising altitude now, so I am now going to switch the seat belt sign off. Feel free to move about as you wish, but please stay inside the plane until we land. It's a bit cold outside, and if you walk on the wings it affects the flight pattern."

After landing: "Thank you for flying Delta Business Express. We hope you enjoyed giving us the business as much as we enjoyed taking you for a ride."

As the plane landed and was coming to a stop at Washington National, a lone voice came over the loudspeaker: "Whoa, big fella. Whoa!"

After a particularly rough landing during thunderstorms in Memphis, a flight attendant on a Northwest flight announced: "Please take care when opening the overhead compartments because, after a landing like that, sure as hell everything has shifted."

From a Southwest Airlines employee: "Welcome aboard Southwest Flight XXX to YYY. To operate your seatbelt, insert the metal tab into the buckle, and pull tight. It works just like every other seatbelt and if you don't know how to operate one, you probably shouldn't be out in public unsupervised. In the event of a sudden loss of cabin pressure, oxygen masks will descend from the ceiling. Stop screaming, grab the mask, and pull it over your face. If you have a small child traveling with you, secure your mask before assisting with theirs. If you are traveling with two small children, decide now which one you love more."

"Weather at our destination is 50 degrees with some broken clouds, but they'll try to have them fixed before we arrive. Thank you, and remember, nobody loves you or your money more than Southwest Airlines."

"Your seat cushions can be used for flotation. In the event of an emergency water landing, please take them with our compliments."

"As you exit the plane, please make sure to gather all of your belongings. Anything left behind will be distributed evenly among the flight attendants. Please do not leave children or spouses."

"Last one off the plane must clean it."

From the pilot during his welcome message: "We are pleased to have some of the best flight attendants in the industry. Unfortunately none of them are on this flight."

A flight attendant's comment on a less than perfect landing: "We ask you to please remain seated as Captain Kangaroo bounces us to the terminal."

Part of a flight attendant's arrival announcement: "We'd like to thank you folks for flying with us today. And, the next time you get the insane urge to go blasting through the skies in a pressurized metal tube, we hope you'll think of us here at US Air.

The Moral is...

An old man, a boy and a donkey were going to town. The boy rode on the donkey and the old man walked. As they traveled along they passed some people who remarked it was a shame the old man was walking and the boy was riding. The man and boy thought maybe they were right, so they changed positions. Later, they passed some people who remarked, "What a shame! He makes that little boy walk."

They then decided they both would walk. Soon they passed some more people who thought out loud that the old man and the boy were stupid to walk when they had a good donkey to ride. So, they both rode the donkey. Now the trio passed some people that shamed them by saying how awful it was to put such a load on a poor donkey.

The boy and man said they were probably right, so they decided to carry the donkey. As they crossed the bridge, they lost their grip on the animal and he fell into the river and drowned.

The moral of the story?

If you try to please everyone, you might as well kiss your ass good-bye.

Honk If You Heard This One

A passenger in a taxi wanted to speak to the driver. He leaned forward and tapped him on the shoulder. The driver screamed, jumped up in the air and yanked the wheel over. The car mounted the curb, demolished a lamppost and came to a stop inches from a shop window.

After things settled, the startled passenger said "I didn't mean to frighten you. I just wanted to ask you a question." The Taxi driver says, "Not your fault, sir. It's my first day as a cab driver... I've been driving a hearse for the past 22 years!"

Okay... It's a Stretch

Long ago lived a seaman named Captain Bravo. His real name was Herschel but he took the name Herman because, you know, he was a manly man's man who showed no fear in facing his enemies. One day, while sailing the seven seas, a lookout spotted a pirate ship and the crew became frantic. Captain Bravo bellowed, "Bring me my red shirt."

The First Mate quickly retrieved the captain's red shirt and while wearing the bright blouse he led his mates into battle and defeated the pirates. Later on, the lookout spotted not one, but two pirate ships. The captain again howled for his red shirt and once again vanquished the pirates.

That evening, all the men sat around on the deck recounting the day's triumphs and one of the them asked the captain: "Sir, why did you call for your red shirt before battle?"

The captain replied: "If I am wounded in the attack, the shirt will not show my blood, and thus, you men will continue to fight, unafraid."

All of the men sat in silence and marveled at the courage of such a manly man. As dawn came the next morning, the lookout once again spotted not one, not two, but TEN pirate ships approaching. The rank and file all stared in worshipful silence at the captain and waited for his usual reply.

Captain Bravo gazed with steely eyes upon the vast armada arrayed against his mighty sailing ship and, without fear, turned, and calmly shouted: "Get me my brown pants."

Section Three: The Kids Have A Word For It

As wonderful humorist Sam Levenson once said, "Insanity is inherited. We get it from our children."

From the Pencil of Babes

A first grade teacher collected well known proverbs. She gave each child in her class the first half of a proverb and asked them to come up with the remainder of the proverb.

Proverb	The add on
Better to be safe than	Punch a 5th grader
Strike while the	Bug is close
It's always darkest before	Daylight Savings
Never underestimate the power of	Termites
You can lead a horse to water but	How?
Don't bite the hand that	Looks dirty
No news is	Impossible
A miss is as good as a	Mister
You can't teach an old dog new	Math
If you lie down with dogs, you'll	Stink in the morning
Love all, trust	Me
The pen is mightier than the	Pigs
An idle mind is	The best way to relax
Where there's smoke there's	Pollution
Happy the bride who	Gets all the presents
A penny saved is	Not much
Two's company, three's	The Musketeers
Don't put off until tomorrow what	You put on to go to bed

A Funny Thing Happened on the Way to the Health Fair

Laugh and the whole world laughs with you, cry and
> You have to blow your nose

None are so blind as   .   Stevie Wonder

Children should be seen and not   Spanked or grounded

If at first you don't succeed,   Get new batteries

You get out of something what you   See pictured on the box

When the blind lead the blind,   Get out of the way

Better late than   Pregnant

The Kids Have All the Answers

A small boy is sent to bed by his father.

Five minutes later: "Da-ad..."

"What?" "I'm thirsty. Can you bring me a drink of water?"

"No. You had your chance. Lights out."

Five minutes later: "Da-aaaad..."

"WHAT?" "I'm THIRSTY...Can I have a drink of water??"

"I told you NO! If you ask again I'll have to spank you!!" Five minutes later.
..
"Daaaa-aaaad..." "WHAT??!!"

"When you come in to spank me, can you bring me a drink of water?"

An exasperated mother, whose son was always getting into mischief, finally asked him, "How do you expect to get into Heaven?" The boy thought it over and said, "Well, I'll just run in and out and in and out and keep slamming the door until St. Peter says, 'For Heaven's sake, Jimmy, come in or stay out!'"

One summer evening during a violent thunderstorm a mother was tucking

29

her small boy into bed. She was about to turn off the light when he asked with a tremor in his voice, "Mommy, will you sleep with me tonight?"

The mother smiled and gave him a reassuring hug. "I can't, dear," she said. "I have to sleep in Daddy's room." A long silence was broken at last by his shaky little voice, "The big sissy."

A mother took her three-year-old daughter to church for the first time. The church lights were lowered, and then the choir came down the aisle, carrying lighted candles. All was quiet until the little one started to sing in a loud voice, "Happy birthday to you. Happy birthday to you..."

Nine-year-old Joey was asked by his mother what he had learned in Sunday School. "Well, Mom, our teacher told us how God sent Moses behind enemy lines on a rescue mission to lead the Israelites out of Egypt. When he got to the Red Sea, he had his engineers build a pontoon bridge, and all the people walked across safely. He used his walkie-talkie to radio headquarters and call in an air strike. They sent in bombers to blow up the bridge and all the Israelites were saved."

"Now, Joey, is that REALLY what your teacher taught you?" his mother asked.
"Well, no, Mom, but if I told it the way the teacher did, you'd never believe it!"

It was that time during the Sunday morning service for "the children's sermon," and all the children were invited to come forward. One little girl was wearing a particularly pretty dress and, as she sat down, the pastor leaned over and said to her, "That is a very pretty dress. Is it your Easter dress?" The little girl replied, directly into the pastor's clip-on microphone, "Yes, and my Mom says it's hell to iron."

Finding one of her students making faces at others on the playground, Ms. Smith stopped to gently reprove the child. Smiling sweetly, the Sunday School teacher said, "Bobby, when I was a child I was told if that I made ugly faces, it would freeze and I would stay like that." Bobby looked up and replied, "Well, Ms Smith, you can't say you weren't warned."

Questions and Answers

How do you decide whom to marry?
You got to find somebody who likes the same stuff. Like, if you like sports, she should like it that you like sports, and she should keep the chips and dip coming. *Alan, age 10*

No person really decides before they grow up whom they're going to marry. God decides it all way before, and you get to find out later who you're stuck with. *Kirsten, age 10*

What is the right age to get married?
Twenty-three is the best age because you know the person FOREVER by then. *Camille, age 10*

No age is good to get married at. You got to be a fool to get married. *Freddie, age 6*

How can a stranger tell if two people are married?
You might have to guess, based on whether they seem to be yelling at the same kids. *Derrick, age 8*

What do you think your mom and dad have in common?
Both don't want any more kids. *Lori, age 8*

What do most people do on a date?
Dates are for having fun, and people should use them to get to know each other. Even boys have something to say if you listen long enough. *Lynnette, age 8*

On the first date, they just tell each other lies, and that usually gets them interested enough to go for a second date. *Martin, age 10*

What would you do on a first date that was turning sour?
I'd run home and play dead. The next day I would call all the newspapers and make sure they wrote about me in all the dead columns. *Craig, age 9*

When is it okay to kiss someone?
When they're rich. *Pam, age 7*

The law says you have to be eighteen, so I wouldn't want to mess with that. *Curt, age 7*

The rule goes like this: If you kiss someone, then you should marry him or her and have kids with them. It's the right thing to do. *Howard, age 8*

Is it better to be single or married?
I don't know which is better, but I'll tell you one thing. I'm never going to have sex with my wife I don't want to be all grossed out. *Theodore, age 8*

It's better for girls to be single but not for boys. Boys need someone to clean up after them. *Anita, age 9*

How would the world be different if people didn't get married?
There sure would be a lot of kids to explain, wouldn't there? *Kelvin, age 8*

How would you make a marriage work?
Tell your wife that she looks pretty even if she looks like a truck. *Ricky, age 10*

The following came from an anonymous mother in Austin, TX

Things I've learned from my children (Honest and No Kidding):

1. A king size waterbed holds enough water to fill a 2,000 sq. foot house 4 inches deep.
2. If you spray hair spray on dust bunnies and run over them with roller blades, they can ignite.
3. A 3-year-old's voice is louder than 200 adults in a crowded restaurant.
4. If you hook a dog leash over a ceiling fan, the motor is not strong enough to rotate a 42-pound boy wearing Batman underwear and a superman cape. It is strong enough, however, to spread paint on all four walls of a 20 X 20 foot room.
5. You should not throw baseballs up when the ceiling fan is on. When using the ceiling fan as a bat, you have to throw the ball up a few times before you get a hit. A ceiling fan can hit a baseball a long way.
6. The glass in windows (even double pane) doesn't stop a baseball hit by a ceiling fan.
7. When you hear the toilet flush and the words "Uh-oh", it's already too late.
8. Brake fluid mixed with Clorox makes smoke, and lots of it.
9. A six-year-old can start a fire with a flint rock even though a 36-year-old man says they can only do it in the movies. A magnifying glass can start a fire even on an overcast day.
10. Certain Legos will pass through the digestive tract of a four-year-old.
11. Play Dough and Microwave should never be used in the same sentence.
12. Super glue is forever.
13. No matter how much Jell-O you put in a swimming pool you still can't walk on water.
14. Pool filters do not like Jell-O.

15. VCR's do not eject Peanut Butter & Jelly sandwiches even though TV commercials show they do.
16. Garbage bags do not make good parachutes.
17. Marbles in gas tanks make lots of noise when driving.
18. You probably do not want to know what that odor is.
19. Always look in the oven before you turn it on. Plastic toys do not like ovens.
20. The fire department in Austin, Texas has a 5-minute response time.
21. The spin cycle on the washing machine does not make earthworms dizzy. It will however make cats dizzy and cats throw up twice their body weight when dizzy.

Math Lesson

Little Tommy was doing very badly in math. His parents had tried everything; tutors, flash cards, special learning centers, in short, everything they could think of. Finally in a last ditch effort, they took enrolled Tommy down in the local Catholic school.

After the first day, little Tommy came home with a very serious look on his face. He didn't kiss his mother hello. Instead, he went straight to his room and started studying. Books and papers were spread out all over the room, and little Tommy was hard at work. His mother was amazed.

She called him down to dinner and to her shock, the minute he was done he marched back to his room without a word and in no time he was back hitting the books as hard as before. This went on for sometime, day after day while the mother tried to understand what made all the difference. Finally, little Tommy brought home his report card. He quietly laid it on the table and went up to his room and hit the books. With great trepidation, his mom looked at it and to her surprise, little Tommy got an A in math.

She could no longer hold her curiosity. She went to his room and said, "Son, what was it? Was it the nuns?" Little Tommy looked at her and shook his head, "No." "Well then," she replied, "was it the books, the discipline, the structure, the uniforms? WHAT was it?"

Little Tommy looked at her and said, "Well, on the first day of school, when I saw that guy on the wall nailed to the big plus sign, I knew they weren't fooling around."

Which Service

One Sunday morning, the pastor noticed little Alex was staring up at the large plaque that hung in the foyer of the church. The plaque was covered with names and small American flags were mounted on either side of it. The seven-year old had been staring at the plaque for some time, so the pastor walked up, stood beside the boy, and said quietly, "Good morning, Alex."

"Good morning, pastor," replied the young man, still focused on the plaque. "Pastor Scheurich what is this?" Alex asked, pointing to the plaque. "Well, son, it's a memorial to all the young men and women who died in the service."

Somberly, they stood together, staring at the large plaque. Little Alex's voice was barely audible when he asked, "Which service, the 8:00 or the 10:30?"

Section Four: This is How Government Works

Government provided the great American humorist Will Rogers with a rich vein of material. This Section simply keeps the tradition alive. The subject is funny until you realize that its happening with our money.

The Explanation of How Government Really Works

A little boy goes to his dad and asks, "What is Politics?"

Dad says, "Well son, let me try to explain it this way: I'm the head of the family, so call me the President. Your mother is the administrator of the money, so we call her the Government.

We're here to take care of your needs, so we'll call you the People. The nanny, we'll consider her the Working Class. And your baby brother, we'll call him the Future. Now think about that and see if it makes sense."

The little boy goes off to bed thinking about what Dad has said. Later that night, he hears his baby brother crying, so he gets up to check on him. He finds that the baby has severely soiled his diaper.

The little boy goes to his parent's room and finds his mother sound asleep. Not wanting to wake her, he goes to the nanny's room. Finding the door locked, he peeks in the keyhole and sees his father in bed with the nanny.

The boy gives up and goes back to bed.

The next morning, the little boy say's to his father, "Dad, I think I understand the concept of politics now."

The father says, "Good, son, tell me in your own words what you think politics is all about."

The little boy replies, "The President is screwing the Working Class while the Government is sound asleep. The People are being ignored and the Future is in deep shit!"

The GI Insurance Plan

Airman Reba was assigned to the induction center, where he advised new recruits about their government benefits, especially their GI insurance.

It wasn't long before Captain Dutterer noticed that Airman Reba was having a staggeringly high success-rate, selling insurance to nearly 100% of the recruits he advised.

Rather than ask about this, the Captain stood in the back of the room and listened to Reba's sales pitch.

Reba explained the basics of the GI Insurance to the new recruits, and then said: "If you have GI Insurance and go into battle and are killed, the government has to pay $200,000 to your beneficiaries. If you don't have GI insurance, and you go into battle and get killed, the government only has to pay a maximum of $6000."

"Now," he concluded, "which group do you think they are going to send into battle first?"

Government Job Pre-requisite

A Redneck walks into a bar with a shotgun in one hand and a bucket of cow manure in the other. He says to the bartender: "Gimme a damn beer!"

The bartender says: "Sure, coming right up." He gets the Redneck a tall draft beer and the guy drinks it down in one gulp, picks up the bucket, throws the manure into the air and blasts it with the shotgun, then he walks out.

Four days later the Redneck returns. He has his shotgun in one hand and another bucket of manure in the other. He walks up to the bar and says to the bartender: "Gimme a damn beer!"

The bartender says: "Whoa, big guy, we're still cleaning up from the last time you were in here. What was that all about, anyway? "

The Redneck says, "I'm in training for job as government employee - drink beer, shoot the shit, and disappear for a few days."

No Nativity in D.C.

The Supreme Court has ruled that there cannot be a nativity scene in Washington, D.C. during the Christmas season. This isn't for any religious constitutional reason. They simply have not been able to find three wise men and a virgin in the Nation's capitol. There was no problem however finding enough asses to fill the stable.

Florida Style Government

FLORIDA: If you think we can't vote, wait 'till you see us drive.

FLORIDA: Home of electile dysfunction.

FLORIDA: We count more than you do.

FLORIDA: If you don't like the way we count, then take I-95 and visit one of the other 56 states.

FLORIDA: We've been Gored by the bull of politics and we're Bushed.

FLORIDA: Relax, Retire, ReVote.

FLORIDA: Viagra voters do it again and again!

FLORIDA: Where your vote counts and counts and counts.

FLORIDA: This is what you get for taking Elian away from us.

FLORIDA: We're number one! Wait! Recount!

        OR:

Palm Beach County: So nice, we let you vote twice.

Palm Beach County: We put the "duh" in Florida.

Sign on I-95 : Florida this way, no that way, 5 miles, wait 10 miles....

In The Government Service

Almost 150 years ago, President Lincoln found it necessary to hire a private investigator, Mr. Alan Pinkerton. He was actually the beginning of the Secret Service.

Since that time federal police authority has grown to a large number of agencies - FBI, CIA, INS, IRS, DEA, BATF, NSA, ATF, etc. Now Congress is considering a proposal for another agency the " Federal Air Transportation Airport Security Service."

Can't you see it now, the new service in their black outfits with their initials in large white letters across their backs?

FATASS

Section Five: Do Blondes Have More Fun?
or
Do We Have More Fun with Blondes?

We pick on Blondes because natural blondes are sweet, loving and gentle, whereas most Brunettes and Redheads hit back.

How Blonde?

She was sooooooooooooooo blonde, that...
..she thought a quarterback was a refund.
..she tried to put M&M's in alphabetical order.
..she thought Boyz II Men was a day care center.
..she thought Eartha Kitt was a set of garden tools.
..she thought General Motors was in the army.
..she thought Meow Mix was a CD for cats.
..she thought TuPac Shakur was a Jewish holiday.
..under "education" on her job application, she put "Hooked On Phonics."
..she tripped over a cordless phone.
..she spent 20 minutes looking at the orange juice can because it said "concentrate."
..at the bottom of the application where it says "sign here," she put "Sagittarius."
..she asked for a price check at the Dollar Store.
..she studied for a blood test.
..she thought she needed a token to get on "Soul Train."
..when she saw the "NC-17, under 17 not admitted", she went home and got 16 friends.
..when she missed the 44 bus, she took the 22 bus twice instead.
..when she went to the airport and saw a sign that said "Airport Left," she
        turned around and went home.
..when she heard that 90% of all crimes occur around the home, she moved.
..she thinks Taco Bell is the Mexican phone company

Arkansas Traveler

A blond from Arkansas is going on his first overseas trip. She drives all the way into Little Rock to apply for a passport. In the passport office, the government official sees that she is visibly puzzled filling his passport application. The passport official looks over his shoulder, and sees the blond trying to write 'twice a week' into the small space labeled SEX.

The official explains: "No, no, no. That is not what we mean by this question. We are asking 'Male' or 'Female'." "Doesn't matter," the blond answers.

Another Blonde - Another Story

A guy took a blonde out on a date one night. Eventually they ended up parked at "Lover's Point" where they started making out. After things started to progress, the guy thought he might get lucky. After a few more minutes of fooling around, he asked his date, "Do you want to get into the back seat?"

"NO!" she answered. Okay, he thought, maybe she's not ready yet.

Now he has her blouse and skirt off and the windows are steamed. Things are getting really hot, so he asks again. "Do you want to get into the back seat?"

"NO!" she answers again. Now he has her bra off, they're both very sweaty, and she even has his pants unzipped. Okay, he thinks, she HAS to want it now. "Do you want to get into the back seat NOW?" he asks again.

"NO!" she answers yet again. Frustrated, he demands, "Well, why not?"

"Because I want to stay up here with you!"

Blonde Mail

A man was in his front yard mowing grass when his attractive blonde female neighbor came out of the house and went straight to the mailbox.

She opened it then slammed it shut stormed back in the house. A little later she came out of her house again went to the mailbox and again opened it, slammed it shut again. Angrily, back into the house she went.

As the man was getting ready to edge the lawn, she came out again, marched to the mailbox, opened it and then slammed it closed harder than ever. Puzzled by her actions the man asked her, "Is something wrong?"

To which she replied," There certainly is!" My stupid computer keeps saying, "YOU'VE GOT MAIL."

The Fishy Blonde

This blonde really wanted to go ice fishing. She'd seen many books on the subject, and finally, after getting all the necessary tools together, she made for the nearest frozen lake. After positioning her comfy footstool, she started to make a circular cut in the ice. Suddenly---from the sky---a voice boomed, "THERE ARE NO FISH UNDER THE ICE!"

Startled, the blonde moved further down the ice, poured a thermos of cappuccino, and began to cut yet another hole. Again, from the heavens, the voice bellowed, "THERE ARE NO FISH UNDER THE ICE!"

The blonde, now quite worried, moved way down to the opposite end of the ice, set up her stool, and tried again to cut her hole. The voice came once more, even louder: "THERE ARE NO FISH UNDER THE ICE!"

She stopped, looked skyward, and said, "Is that you, Lord?"

The voice replied, "NO, THIS IS THE RINK MANAGER!"

The Used Car

A blonde was trying to sell her old car. She was having a lot of problems selling it, because the car had almost 275,000 miles on it.

One day, she told her problem to a brunette she worked with at a salon. The brunette told her, "It may be possible to make the car easier to sell, but it's not legal."

"That doesn't matter," replied the blonde, "if I can only sell the car."

"Okay," said the brunette. "Here is the address of a friend of mine. He owns a car repair shop. Tell him I sent you and he will 'fix it'. Then you shouldn't have a problem anymore trying to sell your car."

The following weekend, the blonde made the trip to the mechanic. About one month later, the brunette asked the blonde, "Did you sell your car?"

"No," replied the blonde, "why should I? It only has 50,000 miles on it!"

Blonde Painter

A blonde decided she could make money by being a "handy person" doing odd jobs and painting. However, she couldn't pick up much business in her blue collar neighborhood.

She decided to try her luck in the ritzy part of town. She spotted a lovely home with a portico and a porch. She stopped her car and knocked on the door. She told the man who answered that she was looking for handy work.

The man asked if she could paint. She said, "I'm a terrific painter. Just point me to the paint."

"How much to paint this porch?"

She said "$25" "$25?" he asked. "Yep! $25."

"Okay," said the man, "You'll find the paint and tarpaulins in the shed out back."

The blonde left, and the man's wife, who over heard the conversation, asked, "Does she realize that the porch goes all around the house?" The man said, "I guess so."

The blonde is back in an hour and half and knocks on the door and announces to the owner that the job is done. "In fact," said the blonde, "I had enough paint to put on a second coat. By the way that's not a Porsche. That's a Ferrari!"

Distant Blonde

A blonde who had been unemployed for several months got a job with the Public Works department in her state. Her job was to paint lines down the center of a rural road.

The supervisor told her that she was on probation and that she must stay at or above the set average of 2 miles per day to keep her job. The blonde agreed to the conditions and starts right away.

The supervisor checking up at the end of the day, found that the blonde had completed 4 miles on her first day, double the average! "Great," he told her, "I think you're really going to work out."

The next day, however, he was disappointed to find that the blonde only accomplished 2 miles. The supervisor thought, "Well she's still at the average and I don't want to discourage her, so I'll just keep quiet." On the third day, the blonde only did one mile and the boss thought, "I need to talk to her before this gets any worse."

The boss brought the new employee to the office and says, "You were doing so great. The first day you did 4 miles, the second day 2 miles, but yesterday you only did one mile. Why? Is there a problem? An injury, equipment failure? What's keeping you from meeting the 2 mile minimum?"

The blonde replied, "Well, each day I keep getting farther and farther away from the paint bucket."

Woof, Woof!

Two blondes were walking down the road and the first blonde said "Look at that dog with one eye!" The other blonde covers one of her eyes and says, "Where?"

Pet Names

What did the Blonde call her pet Zebra?
Spot

Protection

A blonde, worried about the HIV crisis, walks into a drugstore and purchases a pack of condoms. "That will be $1.08, please," says the clerk.

"What's the 8 cents for?" asks the blonde. "It says one dollar right here on the packaging."

"Tax," replies the clerk.

"Gee," says the blonde, "I thought you just rolled them on and they stayed put."

Blonde Phone Call

A blonde with two red ears went to her doctor. The doctor asked her what had happened to her ears She answered, "I was ironing a shirt and the phone rang, but instead of picking up the phone I accidentally picked up the iron and stuck it to my ear."

"Oh, Dear!" the doctor exclaimed in disbelief. "But what happened to your other ear?"

"The son-of-a-bitch called back!"

The Interview

An executive was interviewing a nervous young blonde women for a position in his company. He wanted to find out something about her personality so he asked, "If you could have a conversation with someone, living or dead, who would it be?" The blonde quickly responded, "The living one."

Compassionate Blonde

One day a blonde went to a sea food restaurant and saw the tank where they kept the lobsters. She took pity on these creatures and hid them in her shopping bag. She then went to the woods to set the poor animals free.

Timeless Blonde

"Excuse me, could you tell me the time?" asked the blonde of a man at a bus stop."Sure. It's three fifteen," he replied with a smile. "Thanks," she said, a puzzled look crossing her face. "You know, it's the weirdest thing I've been asking that question all day long, and each time I get a different answer."

Blonde TGIF

A guy enters an elevator already occupied by a blonde. The blonde greeted the guy with "T-G-I-F." He smiled at her and said, "S - H - I - T.

She looked at him, puzzled, and said again, "T - G - I - F."

He acknowledged her remark once more by answering, "S - H - I -T."

The blonde was trying to be friendly and she smiled her biggest smile and said sweetly as possibly, "T - G - I - F "one more time.

The man smiled back at her and once again replied with a quizzical, "S - H - I - T."

Exasperated the blonde, finally decided to explain, "T - G - I - F means Thank Goodness It's Friday, get it?"

He answered back, "S -H - I - T ... Sorry, Honey, It's Thursday!"

Section Six: Medical Moments

Will a laugh a day keep the Doctor away? This section may help us prove a point.

Just Once More

Irving returns from the doctor and tells his wife that the doctor has told him he has only 24 hours to live. Given this prognosis, Irving asks his wife for sex. Naturally, she agrees, and they make love and fall asleep.

About two hours later, the husband nudges his wife and says, "Honey, you know I now have only six hours to live. Could we please do it one more time?"

The wife agrees, and they do it again.

Irving tosses and turns and can't fall asleep. He looks at his watch and realizes that he now has only four hours left. He touches his wife's shoulder and asks, "Honey, please . . .just one more time before I die." She says, "Of course, Dear." They make love for the third time.

After this session, the wife rolls over and falls asleep. Irving, however, worried about his impending death, tosses and turns, until he's down to two more hours. He taps his wife, who rouses.

"Honey, I have only two more hours. Do you think we could . . . At this point the wife sits up and says, "Listen, Irving, I have to get up in the morning... You don't!"

Apart

A couple, Henry and Mary Sue, had been married for 70 years and had made love to each other every day of their married life.. The man, in his 90s, began having chest pains when they made love. The couple went to the doctor. After a careful examination, the doctor told the couple, "I'm afraid that your love making days are over. Henry, your heart can't stand the exertion that comes with love making."

On the way home, the couple discussed how they were going to handle their nightly sexual urges. They decided that the only way to do this was to sleep in separate beds. The couple had a small house, and they decided that Mary Sue would sleep upstairs in the bedroom and Henry would sleep downstairs on the sofa.

Henry has tossed and turned until 1 a.m. when he couldn't stand it anymore. He got off the sofa, and started up the stairs. About half way up the stairs he was startled to see Mary Sue coming down the stairs.

She said. "Henry, what are you doing?"
He said, "I'm coming up the stairs to die. What are you doing?"

She said, "I was going down the stairs to kill you."

The Hospital: Sometimes the truth is more amusing than fiction...

A man comes into the ER and yells "My wife's going to have her baby in the cab!"
The ER physician grabs his stuff, rushes out to the cab, lifts the lady's dress, and begins to take off her underwear. Suddenly he notices that there are several cabs, and he's in the wrong one.

One day I had to be the bearer of bad news when I told a wife that her husband had died of a massive myocardial infarct. Not more than five minutes later, I heard her reporting to the rest of the family that he had died of a "massive internal fart."

I was performing a complete physical, including the visual acuity test. I placed the patient twenty feet from the chart and began, "Cover your right eye with your hand." He read the 20/20 line perfectly. "Now your left." Again, a flawless read. "Now both," I requested. There was silence.
He couldn't even read the large E on the top line. I turned and discovered that he had done exactly what I had asked; he was standing there with both his eyes covered. I was laughing too hard to finish the exam.

A nurses' aide was helping a patient into the bathroom when the patient exclaimed, "You're not coming in here with me. "This is a one-seater!"

During a patient's two week follow-up appointment with his cardiologist, he informed his doctor that he was having trouble with one of his medications.

"Which one?", asked the doctor.

"The patch. The nurse told me to put on a new one every six hours and now I'm running out of places to put it!"

The doctor had him quickly undress and discovered what he hoped he wouldn't see. The man had over fifty patches on his body! Now the instructions include removal of the old patch before applying a new one.

While acquainting myself with a new elderly patient, I asked, "How long have you been bedridden?" After a look of complete confusion she answered, "Why, not for about twenty years when my husband was alive."

A nurse caring for a woman from Kentucky asked, "So how's your breakfast this morning?" "It's very good, except for the Kentucky Jelly. I can't seem to get used to the taste," the patient replied. The nurse asked to see the jelly and the woman produced a foil packet labeled "KY Jelly."

Generics

In pharmacology all drugs have a generic name.
Tylenol is Acetaminophen
Advil is Ibuprofen.
Rogaine is Minoxidil, and so on.

The FDA has been looking for a generic name for Viagra and has announced that they have settled on Mycoxafloppin.

Over the past few years more money has been spent on breast implants and Viagra than on Alzheimer's. In a few years we will have a lot of people running around with huge breasts and big erections who don't remember what to do with them.

Inner Peace

I think I've found inner peace.

My therapist told me a way to achieve inner peace was to finish things I had started. Today I finished two bags of potato chips, a lemon pie, a fifth of Jack Daniel's and a small box of chocolate candy.

I feel better already. Pass this along to those who need it.

Mis-Diagnosis

A disheveled man, who was obviously drunk and reeked with the smell of booze, sat down on a subway seat next to a priest. The man's shirt was stained, his face was plastered with red lipstick, and a half empty bottle of gin was sticking out of his torn coat pocket.

He opened his newspaper and began reading. After a few minutes the man turned to the priest and asked, "Say, Father, what causes arthritis?"

"My son, it's caused by loose living, being with cheap, wicked women, too much alcohol and a contempt for your fellow man, sleeping around with prostitutes and a lack of bathing."

"Well, I'll be damned," the drunk muttered, returning to his paper.

The priest, thinking about what he had said, nudged the man and apologized. "I'm very sorry. I didn't mean to come on so strong. How long have you had arthritis?"

"I don't have it, Father. I was just reading here that the Pope does."

What Luck

The woman's husband had been slipping in and out of a coma for several months, yet she had stayed by his hospital bedside every single day. One day, he came out of the coma and he motioned for her to come nearer. As she sat by him, he whispered, his eyes full of tears, "You have been with me all through the bad times. When I got fired, you were there to support me. When my business failed, you were there. When I got shot, you were by my side. When we lost the house, you stayed right here. When my health started failing, you were still by my side...You know what?"

"What dear?" She gently asked, smiling as her heart began to fill with warmth.

"I think you're bad luck."

The Price of a Brain

In the hospital the relatives gathered in the waiting room, where their family member lay gravely ill.

Finally, the doctor came in looking tired and somber. "I'm afraid I'm the bearer of bad news," he said as he surveyed the worried faces. "The only hope left for your loved one at this time is a brain transplant. It's an experimental procedure, semi-risky and you will have to pay for the brain yourselves."

The family members sat silent as they absorbed the news. After a great length of time, someone asked, "Well, how much does a brain cost?"

The doctor responded, "$5,000 for a male brain, and $200 for a female brain." The moment turned awkward. Men in the room tried not to smile, avoiding eye contact with the women, but some were smirking.

A male family member, unable to control his curiosity, blurted out the question everyone wanted to ask, "Why is the male brain cost so much more?" The doctor smiled at the childish innocence and answered, "It's just standard pricing procedure. We have to mark down the price of the female brains, because they've actually been used."

The Check-up

A woman accompanied her husband to the doctor's office. After his check-up, the doctor called the wife into his office alone.

He said, "Your husband is suffering from a very severe disease, which is aggravated by his horrible stress. If you don't do the following, your husband will surely die:

Each morning, fix him a healthy breakfast. Be pleasant and make sure he is in a good mood.

For lunch make him a nutritious meal he can take to work. And for dinner, prepare an especially nice meal for him. Don't burden him with chores, as this could further his stress. Don't discuss your problems with him; it will only make his stress worse. Try to relax your husband in the evening by wearing lingerie and giving him plenty of back rubs. Encourage him to watch some type of team sporting event on television.

And, most importantly make love with your husband several times a week and satisfy his every whim. If you can do this for the next 10 months to a year, I think your husband will regain his health completely."

On the way home, the husband asked his wife, "What did the doctor say?"

His wife replied, "You're going to die."

Elective Surgery

A middle-aged woman had a heart attack and was taken to the hospital. While on the operating table she had a near-death experience. Seeing God, she asked if this was it.

God said, "No, you have another 43 years, 2 months, and 8 days to live."

Since she had so much more time to live, she figured she might as well make the most of it. Upon recovery, the woman decided to stay in the hospital and have a facelift, liposuction, breast augmentation, tummy tuck, etc. She even had a hair stylist come in and change her hair color.

She got out of the hospital after the last operation, and while crossing the street was killed by an ambulance speeding to the hospital.

Arriving in front of God, she demanded, "I thought you said I had another 40 years?"

God replied, "I didn't recognize you.

Thank God

At a nursing home in Miami, Florida, a group of Senior Citizens were sitting around talking about their ailments:
"My arms are so weak I can hardly lift this cup of coffee," said one.

"Yes, I know. My cataracts are so bad I can't even see my coffee," replied another.

"I can't turn my head because of the arthritis in my neck," said a third, to which several nodded weakly in agreement.

"My blood pressure pills make me dizzy,".... another went on.

"I guess that's the price we pay for getting old," winced an old man as he slowly shook his head.

Then there was a short moment of silence.

"Well, it's not that bad," said one woman cheerfully. "Thank God we can all still drive."

Section Seven: Body Parts

I've been laughing at body parts ever since I looked in a mirror.

Once Upon A Time

In the hospital, a nurse at the beginning of the shift places her stethoscope on an elderly and slightly deaf female patient's anterior chest wall. "Big breaths," instructed the nurse. "Yes, they used to be," said the patient with remorse.

I Don't Know...

A drunk is sitting at a bar in a restaurant when he spies, via a mirror, a woman entering. The woman, who makes Dolly Parton look as if she had the contours of a boy, stood near the doorway as if she was waiting for someone.

Gazing at the gargantuan bust, of this well dressed, dignified woman, the drunk blurts out "I don't think her boobs are real. They're too big to be real. No, no, they can't be real."

The woman's face turns red and she turns away from him. The drunk stumbles off his ball stool and staggers over the lady. He says, "I'll give you $10,000 if you let me touch your boobs to see if they are real!" She turns further away from him, but he sidles up to her and repeats, "I'll give you $10,000 if you let me touch your boobs to see if they are real!"

At this point you can see from the expression on her face that the gears are turning in her mind. She then says, "Do you expect me to get undressed?" The drunks says, "Oh, no. I just want to feel under your bra to if they're real and I'll give you $10,000.

"$10,000 dollars?"

"10, 000 dollars!"

"Okay," she says, "Let's go over there." The drunk and the woman go to a secluded area of the restaurant behind a column. The woman turned her back to the open area of the restaurant and unbuttons her blouse.

The drunk, obviously at work, says, "I don't know? I just don't know? I don't know?" Indignantly the woman asks, "You mean to tell me with all that groping you don't know if my breasts are real?"

The drunk says, "I don't know where I'm going get the $10,000."

The Boss

All the organs of the body were having a meeting, trying to decide who should be in charge.

"I should be in charge," said the brain, "because I run all the body's systems, so without me nothing would happen."

"I should be in charge," said the blood, "because I circulate oxygen all over, so without me you'd all waste away."

"I should be in charge," said the stomach, "because I process food and give all of you energy."

"I should be in charge" said the legs, "because I carry the body wherever it needs to go."

"I should be in charge" said the eyes, "because I allow the body to see where it goes."

"I should be in charge," said the rectum, "because I'm responsible for waste removal." All the other body parts laughed at the rectum and fired off insults!

In a huff, the rectum shut down tight. Within a few days, the brain had a terrible headache, the stomach was bloated, the legs got wobbly, the eyes got watery and the blood was toxic. They all decided that the rectum should be the boss.

The moral of the story?

You don't have to be important to be in charge... you just have to be an asshole!

Spouting Off

Barry enters a public washroom and has to use the only available urinal, between two elderly men. Always curious, he glances to his left and sees the guy pissing, but there are two streams.

"What the hell is that?" Barry asks.

"War wound. I took a bullet in the penis in North Africa. They were able to save my dick but they had to leave two holes"

Then Barry looks to his right and sees. . . three streams !!!

"What the hell is that?"

"War wound. German shell... shrapnel hit the penis, left three holes"

The two veterans then look over at Barry in the middle and see. . . 12 streams!!

"War wound??"

"No, my zipper's stuck"

The Hokey Pokey

There was very sad news when the funeral home employees tried to put Larry LaPrise, a Detroit native who wrote the song "Hokey Pokey", died. They had an especially difficult time trying to keep him in the casket. They'd put his left leg in and ...well, you know the rest.

The Finger

Before the Battle of Agincourt in 1415, the French, anticipating victory over the English, proposed to cut off the middle finger of all captured English soldiers. Without the middle finger it would be impossible to draw the renowned English longbow and therefore be incapable of fighting in the future.

This famous weapon was made of the native English Yew tree, and the act of drawing the longbow was known as "plucking the yew" (or "pluck yew").

Much to the bewilderment of the French, the English won a major upset and began mocking the French by waving their middle fingers at the defeated French, saying, "See, we can still pluck yew! PLUCK YEW!"

Since 'pluck yew' is rather difficult to say, the difficult consonant cluster at the beginning has gradually changed to a labiodental fricative 'F', and thus the words often used in conjunction with the one-finger-salute are mistakenly thought to have something to do with an intimate encounter.

It is also because of the pheasant feathers on the arrows used with the longbow that the symbolic
gesture is known as "giving the bird".

A Short Complaint

A midget complained to his doctor that his testicles ached all the time. The physician told the midget to drop his pants. The doctor then lifted him up onto the table to take a look. Putting one finger under the left testicle, the doctor had the midget cough. "Hmmm..." said the doctor.

Then, putting his finger under the right testicle, the doc asked the midget to cough again. "Ahhh!" said the doctor, as he reached for his surgical scissors. Snip, snip, snip on the right side and then snip, snip, snip on the left side.

The doctor then told the midget to pull up his pants and see if he still ached. The midget was delighted with the result. He walked around the doc's office and his testicles did not ache. "What did you do Doc?" he asked.

The doc replied, "I cut two inches off the top of your cowboy boots."

Infantile

Jim decided to propose to Sandy, but prior to her acceptance, Sandy had to confess to her man about her childhood illness.

She informed Jim that she suffered a disease that left her breasts the size of a 12 year old's.

He stated that it was okay, because he loved her so much. However, Jim felt this was the time for him to open up and admit that he also had a deformity.

Jim looked Sandy in the eyes and said, "I too have a problem. My penis is the same size as an infant, and I hope you can deal with that once we are married."

She said, "Yes, I will marry you and learn to live with your infant sized penis."

Sandy and Jim got married and they could not wait for the honeymoon.

Jim rushed Sandy off to their hotel suite and they started touching, teasing and holding one another.

As Sandy put her hands in Jim's pants, she began to scream and ran out of the room!

Jim ran after her to find out what was wrong. She said, "You told me your penis was the size of an infant!"

"It is," he said, "8 lbs. 7 oz.. and 19 inches long."

The Amazing Goldstein

A traveling salesman comes to a small town in the Midwest and notices a circus banner. "**Don't Miss the Amazing Goldstein!**" Curious, the salesman buys a ticket, and sits through the usual circus acts; the animals, clowns, contortionists, etc.

Finally, the trumpets blare, and all eyes turn to the center ring! There, positioned on top of this table are three walnuts. Entering into center ring is a little old Jewish man, no more than 5 feet tall, barely able to make his way to the table.

He clumsily unzips his pants, and whips out his unusually long organ, and with 3 mighty swings, proceeds to smash all three walnuts! The crowd goes wild with thunderous applause! "**The Amazing Goldstein**" is then carried off by the clowns.

20 years later, the same salesman arrives in a nearby town and he notices a faded sign for that very same circus, and the same "**Don't Miss the Amazing Goldstein!**" The salesman can't believe the old guy is still alive, much less still doing his act! Once more he buys his ticket, sits through the usual circus acts, and again the center ring is illuminated, but this time, there sits three coconuts on top of a table.

Little old Goldstein takes forever to make his way to the table, but upon reaching his destination, he smashes the coconuts with 3 swings of his unique and celebrated mighty organ. The salesman just can believe his eyes, and requests a meeting with "**The Amazing Goldstein**" after the show. In the dressing room, he tells Goldstein he's never seen anything like his act in the whole, wide world.

Then salesman asks, "But WHY are you now smashing coconuts, instead of the much easier and smaller walnuts?"

"The Amazing Goldstein" replies, "My eyes aren't what they used to be!"

Striving to be the Fastest

The newly born sperm was receiving instructions in conception from the teacher. "As soon as you hear the siren, run for the tunnel and swim in a straight line until you get to the entrance of a damp cavern. At the end of the cavern you will find a red, sticky ball which is the egg. Address it and say, 'I'm a Sperm.' She will answer, 'I'm an Egg.' From that moment on you will work together to create the embryo. Do you understand?"

The sperm nodded affirmatively.

Two days later, the sperm is taking a nap when he hears the siren. He wakes immediately and swims to the tunnel. A multitude of sperm swim behind him. He knows he has to arrive first. When he nears the entrance to the cavern, he looks back and sees that he is far ahead of the other sperm. He is able to swim at a slower pace but does approach the red, sticky ball in front..

When, at last, he reaches the red, sticky ball, he smiles and says, "Hi, I'm a sperm!"

The red sticky ball smiles and says, "Hi. I'm a tonsil."

When It's Over It's Over

My nookie days are over,
My pilot light is out,
What used to be my sex appeal,
Is now my water spout.

Time was when, on its own accord,
From my trousers it would spring,
But now I've got a full-time job,
To find the blasted thing.

It used to be embarrassing,
The way it would behave,

For every single morning,
It would stand and watch me shave.

Now as old age approaches,
It sure gives me the blues,
To see it hang its little head,
And watch me tie my shoes!

Request for a Pay Raise

Dear Management,
I, the penis, hereby request a raise in salary for the following reasons:
I do physical labor
I work at great depths
I plunge head first into everything I do
I do not get weekends or public holidays off
I work in a damp environment
I don't get paid overtime
I work in a dark workplace that has poor ventilation
I work in high temperatures
Sincerely,
The Penis

Dear Penis,
After assessing your request, and considering the arguments you have raised, the administration rejects your request for the following reasons:
You do not work 8 hours straight
You fall asleep on the job after brief work periods
You do not always follow the orders of the management team
You do not stay in your allocated position, and often visit other areas
You do not take initiative - you need to be pressured and stimulated in order to start working
You leave the workplace rather messy at the end of your shift
You don't always observe necessary safety regulations, such as wearing the correct protective clothing
You'll retire well before reaching 65
You're unable to work double shifts
You sometimes leave your allocated position before you have completed the day's work
And if that were not all, you have been seen constantly entering and leaving the workplace carrying 2 suspicious looking bags.
Sincerely,
The Management

Section Eight: Age is Only a State of Mind

If you have to grow older (and you have to), you might as well do it laughing! It will annoy the hell out of everyone around you.

Why Not?

A grandfather finds a bottle of Viagra in his grandson's medicine cabinet. He asks his grandson about using one of the pills and the grandson says, "I don't think you should take one; they're very strong and very expensive.""What do they cost?" asks the grandfather. "$10.00 a pill," answers the grandson.

"I don't care," says grandpop , "I'd like to try one and I'll leave the money on your pillow as soon as I break this $20.00 bill."

After the grandson came home from work the next day, he finds $110.00 on his pillow. He says to his grandfather , "I told you each pill was $10.00, not $110.00."

"I know," says Granddad, "the extra hundred is from your grandmother."

Bragging Rights

An elderly gent goes into confession and says to the priest, "Father, I'm 80 years old, a widower, have four kids and 11 grandchildren, and last night I had an affair. I made love to two 18 year old girls. Both of them. Twice!"

The priest said: "Well, my son, when was the last time you were in confession?"

"Never, Father. I'm Jewish," replied the man.

"So then, why are you telling me?"

"I'm telling everybody!"

Only Social Security?

A retired gentleman went into the social security office to apply for Social Security.

After waiting in line a long time he got to the counter. The woman behind the counter asked him for his driver's license to verify his age.

He checked his pockets and realized he had left his wallet at home. He told the woman that he was very sorry, but he seemed to have left his wallet at home.

"Will I have to go home and come back now?" he asked.

The woman says, "Unbutton your shirt."

So he opens his shirt revealing lots of curly silver hair. She says, "That silver hair on your chest is proof enough for me," and she processed his Social Security application.

When he gets home, the man excitedly tells his wife about his experience at the Social Security office. She said, "You should have dropped your pants, you might have qualified for disability too."

Old Is...

"Old is when".... Your sweetie says, "Lets go upstairs and make love," and you answer, "Honey, I can't do both!"

Old is when"....Your friends compliment you on your new alligator shoes and you're barefoot.

"Old is when".... A sexy babe catches your fancy and your pacemaker opens the garage door.

"Old is when".... Going bra-less pulls all the wrinkles out of your face.

"Old is when".... You don't care where your spouse goes, just as long as you don't have to go along.

"Old is when"....When you are cautioned to slow down by the doctor instead of by the police.

"Old is when".... "Getting a little action" means I don't need to take any fiber today.

"Old is when".... "Getting lucky" means you find your car in the parking lot.

"Old is when".... An "all nighter" means not getting up to pee!

The Anniversary

An elderly couple were celebrating their 50th wedding anniversary, so they decided to return to the little town where they first met. They sat in a small coffee shop in the town and were telling the waitress about their love for each other and how they met at this same spot.

Sitting in the booth next to them was the local cop and he smiled as the old couple spoke. After the waitress left the table, the old man said to his wife,"Remember the first time we made love, it was up in that field across the road, when I put you against the fence. Why don't we do it again for old times sake? The wife giggled and said, "Sure, why not."

Off they went out the door and across to the field. The cop smiled to himself, thinking how romantic this was and decided he better keep an eye on the couple so they didn't run into any harm. The old couple walked to the field and as they approached the fence they began to undress. The old man picked up his wife when they were naked and leaned her against the fence. The cop was watching from the bushes and was surprised at what he saw.

With the vitality of youth, the wife bounced up and down excitedly, while the husband thrashed around like a wild man, then they both fell to the ground in exhaustion.

Eventually, they stood up, shook themselves, and got dressed. As they walked back towards the road, the cop stepped from his hiding spot and said, "I really wasn't spying,. I wanted to make sure no harm came to you. But, that is the most wonderful love making I have ever seen. You must have been a wild couple when you were young."

"Not really," said the old man, "when we were young, that fence wasn't electric."

Now that I'm older, here's what I've discovered:

1. I started out with nothing, and I still have most of it.

2. My wild oats have turned into prunes and All Bran.

3. I finally got my head together- now my body is falling apart.

4. Funny, I don't remember being absent minded.

5. All reports are in; life is now officially unfair.

6. If all is not lost, where is it?

7. It is easier to get older than it is to get wiser.

8. Some days you're the dog; some days the hydrant.

9. I wish the buck stopped here; I sure could use a few.

10. Kids in the back seat of a car cause accidents.

11. Accidents in the back seat of a car cause...kids.

12. It's hard to make a comeback when you haven't been anywhere.

13. Only time the world beats a path to your door is when you're in the bathroom.

14. If God wanted me to touch my toes, he would have put them on my knees.

15. When I'm finally holding all the cards, why does everyone decide to play chess?

16. It's not hard to meet expenses...they're everywhere.

17. The only difference between a rut and a grave is the depth.

18. These days, I spend a lot of time thinking about the hereafter... I go somewhere to get something, and then wonder what I'm here after?

How old is Grandpa?

Stay with this -- the answer is at the end -- it blew me away. How old is Grandpa?

One evening a grandson was talking to his grandfather about current events. The grandson asked his grandfather what he thought about the shootings at schools, the computer age, and just things in general.

The granddad replied, "Well, let me think a minute, I was born, before television, penicillin, polio shots, frozen foods, Xerox, contact lenses, Frisbees and the pill. There was no radar, credit cards, laser beams or ball-point pens. Man had not invented pantyhose, air conditioners, dishwashers, clothes dryers, and the clothes were hung out to dry in the fresh air and man hadn't yet walked on the moon. Your grandmother and I got married first - and then lived together. Every family had a father and a mother.

"Until I was 25, I called every man older than I, 'Sir' - and after I turned 25, I still called policemen and every man with a title, 'Sir.' We were before gay-rights, computer-dating, dual careers, daycare centers, and group therapy. Our lives were governed by the Ten Commandments, good judgment, and common sense. We were taught to know the difference between right and wrong and to stand up and take responsibility for our actions. Serving your country was a privilege; living in this country was a bigger privilege

"We thought fast food was what people ate during Lent. Having a meaningful relationship meant getting along with your cousins. Draft dodgers were people who closed their front doors when the evening breeze started. Time-sharing meant time the family spent together in the evenings and weekends - not purchasing condominiums. We never heard of tape decks, CDs, electric typewriters, yogurt, or guys wearing earrings. We listened to the Big Bands, Jack Benny, and the President's speeches on our radios. And I don't ever remember any kid blowing his brains out listening to Tommy Dorsey.

If you saw anything with 'Made in Japan' on it, it was junk. The term 'making out' referred to how you did on your school exam. Pizza Hut, McDonald's, and instant coffee were unheard of. We had 5 & and 10-cent stores where you could actually buy things for 5 and 10 cents. Ice cream cones, phone calls, rides on a streetcar, and a Pepsi were all a nickel. And if you didn't want to splurge, you could spend your nickel on enough stamps to mail 1 letter and 2 postcards.

"You could buy a new Chevy Coupe for $600 but who could afford one? Too bad, because gas was 11 cents a gallon. In my day, 'grass' was mowed, 'coke' was a cold drink, 'pot' was something your mother cooked in, and 'rock music' was your grandmother's lullaby. 'Aids' were helpers in the Principal's office, 'chip' meant a piece of wood, 'hardware' was found in a hardware store, and 'software' wasn't even a word. And we were the last generation to actually believe that a lady needed a husband to have a baby. No wonder people call us "old and confused" and say there is a generation gap.

... and how old do you think I am ???

This man would be only 58 years old! (In 2002)

True Love

At 85 years, Frank marries a lovely 25 year old woman. Because her new husband is so old the woman decides that on their wedding night they should have separate bedrooms. She is concerned that the old fellow could overexert himself.

After the wedding festivities she prepares herself for bed and for the knock on the door she is expecting. Sure enough the knock comes and there is her 85 year old groom ready for action.

They unite in conjugal union and all goes well, whereupon he takes his leave of her and she prepares to go to sleep for the night.

After an hour later there's a knock on the door and there old Frank is again ready for more action. Somewhat surprised she consents to further coupling, which is again successful.

The octogenarian once again bids her a fond good night and leaves. She is certainly ready for slumber at this point, and, after a few more minutes, is close to sleep.

An hour later and for the third time there is a knock at the door and there he is again -- fresh as a 25 year old and ready for more. Again they ravish one another.

As they're basking in the afterglow the young bride says to him, "I am thoroughly impressed that at your age you have enough juice to go at it three times. I've been with guys less than half your age who were only good for one time. You're a great lover, Frank."

Frank, looking quite confused, turns to her and asks, "You mean I was here already?"

4 Stages of Life

1. You believe in Santa Claus.
2. You don't believe in Santa Claus.
3. You are Santa Claus.

4. You look like Santa Claus.

Great Truths about Growing Old

Growing old is mandatory; growing up is optional.

Insanity is my only means of relaxation.

Forget the health food. I need all the preservatives I can get.

You're getting old when you get the same sensation from a rocking chair that you once got from a roller coaster.

Perhaps you know why women over fifty don't have babies: They would put them down somewhere and forget they left them.

Every time I think about exercise, I lie down till the thought goes away.

It's frustrating when you know all the answers, but nobody bothers to ask you the questions.

There cannot be a crisis this week; my schedule is already full.

Time may be a great healer, but it's also a lousy beautician.

Age doesn't always bring wisdom. Sometimes age comes alone.

Just when I was getting used to yesterday, along came today.

Sometimes I think I understand everything, then I regain consciousness

It is bad to suppress laughter; it goes back down and spreads to your hips.

Freedom of the press means no-iron clothes.

Seen it all, done it all, can't remember most of it.

Discovery

Two elderly men were eating breakfast in a restaurant one morning.

One noticed something funny about his friend's ear. . He asked, "Why do you have a suppository in your left ear?"

"What?"

"Do you know you've got a suppository in your left ear?"

"I have a suppository?"

He pulled it out and stared at it. "Ah, ha... Now I think I know where my hearing aid is."

The Nursing Home

An old man and an old woman used to sit in the nursing home all day watching television together.

The old woman would sit there holding the old man's pretzel. The nursing staff tried to get them to stop but they couldn't and decided to leave them alone. Since they weren't hurting anyone, they just put a blanket over the couples' lap and kind of ignored it.

But one day the old man didn't show up and when the old woman saw him in the dining hall later that evening she asked, "Where were you today?"

"I watched TV with Becky today," he said quite matter-of- factly.

With slight cynicism in her voice, the old woman said, "What's she got that I don't have."

The old man paused and said, "Parkinson's."

Edited by Fred Neil

Section Nine: Sex and the Sexes

It is not men against women or vice versa. It is us against what comes naturally. Enjoy!

The Mood Ring

My husband bought me a mood ring the other day.....

When I'm in a good mood, it turns green. When I'm in a bad mood, it leaves a red mark on his forehead.

Switch

HUSBAND: Shall we try a different position tonight?

WIFE: That's a good idea. Why don't you stand at the sink and do the dishes and I'll sit on the sofa and fart.

Horsing Around

A guy is sitting quietly reading his paper when his wife sneaks up behind him and whacks him on the head with a frying pan.

"What was that for?" he says.

"That was for the piece of paper in your pants pocket with the name Mary Lou written on it," she replies.

"Two weeks ago when I went to the races, Mary Lou was the name of one of the horses I bet on," he explains

She looks satisfied and apologizes.

Three days later he's again sitting in his chair reading when she nails him with an even bigger frying pan, knocking him out cold. When he comes to . he says, "What the hell was that for?

"Your horse called. "

Whose Phone?

There are several men in the locker room of a private club after exercising. Suddenly a cell phone that was on one of the benches rings. A man picks

it up and the following conversation
ensues:

- Hello?

- Honey, It's me.

- Sugar!

- Are you at the club?

- Yes.

- Great! I am at the mall two blocks from where you are. I saw a beautiful mink coat... It is absolutely gorgeous!! Can I buy it?

- What's the price?

- Only $12,500.00

- Well, OK, go ahead and get it if you like it that much...

- Ahhh and I also stopped by the Mercedes dealership and saw the 2002 models. I saw one I really liked. I spoke with the salesman and he gave me a really good price ... and since we need to exchange the BMW that we bought last year...

- What price did he quote you?

- Only $70,000...

- OK, but for that price I want it with all the options.

- Great!, before we hang up, something else...

- What?

- I was reconciling your bank account and... I stopped by the real estate agent this morning and I saw the house we had looked at last year ... it's for sale!! Remember? The one with a pool, English Garden, acre of park area, beachfront property...

- How much are they asking?

- Only $7,950,000... a magnificent price, and I see that we have enough in the bank to cover the down payment...

- Well, than go ahead and buy it, but just bid $7,500,000. OK?

- OK, sweetie... Thanks! I'll see you later!! I love you!!!

- Bye... I do too...

The man hangs up, closes the phone's flap and raises his hand while holding the phone aloft and asks to all those present:

- Does anyone know who this phone belongs to?

The Perfect Gift

Dear Diary...
For my fiftieth birthday this year, my husband (the dear) purchased a week of personal training at the local health club for me. Although I am still in great shape, I decided it would be a good idea to go ahead and give it a try.

I called the club and made my reservations with a personal trainer, Bruce, who identified himself as a 26 year old aerobics instructor and model for athletic clothing and swim wear. My husband seemed pleased with my enthusiasm to get started. The club encouraged me to keep a diary to chart my progress.

MONDAY: Started my day at 6:00am. Tough to get out of bed, but found it was well worth it when I arrived at the health club to find Bruce waiting for me. He is something of a Greek god - with blond hair, dancing eyes and a dazzling white smile. Woo Hoo!!

Bruce gave me a tour and showed me the machines. He took my pulse after five minutes on the treadmill. He was alarmed that my pulse was so fast, but I attribute it to standing next to him in his Lycra aerobic outfit.

I enjoyed watching the skillful way in which he conducted his aerobics class after my workout today. Very inspiring. Bruce was encouraging as I did my sit-ups, although my gut was already aching from holding it in the whole time he was around. This is going to be a FANTASTIC week!!

 TUESDAY: I drank a whole pot of coffee, but I finally made it out the door. Bruce made me lie on my back and push a heavy iron bar into the air then he put weights on it! My legs were a little wobbly on the treadmill, but made the full mile. Bruce's rewarding smile made it all worthwhile. I feel GREAT!! It's a whole new life for me.

WEDNESDAY: The only way I can brush my teeth is by laying on the toothbrush on the counter and moving my mouth back and forth over it. I believe I have a hernia in both pectorals. Driving was OK as long as I didn't try to steer or stop. I parked on top of a GEO in the club parking lot. Bruce was impatient with me, insisting that my screams bothered other club members. His voice is a little too perky for early in the morning and when he scolds, he gets this nasally whine that is VERY annoying. My chest hurt when I got on the treadmill, so Bruce put me on the stair monster. Why the hell would anyone invent a machine to simulate a activity rendered obsolete by elevators? Bruce told me it would help me get in shape and enjoy life. He said some other shit too.

THURSDAY: Bruce was waiting for me with his vampire-like teeth exposed as his thin, cruel lips were pulled back in a full snarl. I couldn't help being a half an hour late, it took me that long to tie my shoes. Bruce took me to work out with dumbbells. When he was not looking, I ran and hid in the men's room. He sent Lars to find me, then, as punishment, put me on the rowing machine - which I sank.

FRIDAY: I hate that bastard Bruce more than any human being has ever hated any other human being in the history of the world. Stupid, skinny, anemic little cheerleader. If there was a part of my body I could move without unbearable pain, I would beat him with it. Bruce wanted me to work on my triceps. I don't have any triceps! And if you don't want dents in the floor, don't hand me the *&%#(#&**!!@*@ barbells or anything that weighs more than a sandwich. (Which I am sure you learned in the sadist school you attended and graduated magna cum laude from.) The treadmill flung me off and I landed on a health and nutrition teacher. Why couldn't it have been someone softer, like the drama coach or the choir director?

SATURDAY: Bruce left a message on my answering machine in his grating, shrilly voice wondering why I did not show up today. Just hearing him made me want to smash the machine with my planner. However, I lacked the strength to even use the TV remote and ended up catching eleven straight hours of the Weather Channel.

SUNDAY: I'm having the Church van pick me up for services today so I can go and thank GOD that this week is over. I will also pray that next year my husband (the middle-aged fart) will choose a gift for me that is fun - like a root canal or a hysterectomy.

The Difference between Men and

Women

Nicknames: If Laura, Suzanne, Debra and Rose go out for lunch, they will call each other Laura, Suzanne, Debra and Rose.

If Mike, Charlie, Bob, and John go out, they will affectionately refer to each other as Fat Boy, Godzilla, Peanut-Head and Scrappy.

Eating Out: When the bill arrives, Mike, Charlie, Bob and John will each throw in $20, even though it's only for $32.50. None of them will have anything smaller, and none will actually admit they want change back.

When the girls get their bill, out come the pocket calculators.

Money: A man will pay $2 for a $1 item he wants. A woman will pay $1 for a $2 item that she doesn't want.

Bathrooms: A man has six items in his bathroom - a toothbrush, comb, shaving cream, razor, a bar of soap, and a towel from the Holiday Inn.

The average number of items in the typical woman's bathroom is 337. A man would not be
able to identify most of these items.

Arguments: A woman has the last word in any argument. Anything a man says after that is the beginning of a new argument.

Cats: Women love cats. Men say they love cats, but when women aren't looking, men kick cats.

Future: A woman worries about the future until she gets a husband. A man never worries about the future until he gets a wife.

Success: A successful man is one who makes more money than his wife can spend. A successful woman is one who can find such a man.

Marriage: A woman marries a man expecting he will change, but he doesn't. A man marries a woman expecting that she won't change and she does.

Dressing Up: A woman will dress up to go shopping, water the plants, empty the garbage, answer the phone, read a book, and get the mail. A man will dress up for weddings and funerals.

Natural: Men wake up as good-looking as they went to bed. Women somehow deteriorate during the night.

Offspring: Ah, children. A woman knows all about her children. She knows about dentist appointments and romances, best friends, favorite foods, secret fears and hopes and dreams.

A man is vaguely aware of some short people living in the house.

What Studies Found

Study #1
A recent study found out which days men prefer to have sex. It was found that men preferred to engage in sexual activity on the days that started with the letter "T" . . ..

Example of those days:
Tuesday
Thursday
Thanksgiving
Today
Tomorrow
Thaturday and Thunday

Study #2
 Why Men Get out of Bed . . .

A recent survey was conducted to discover why men get out of bed in the middle of the night. The results were as follows:

5% said it was to get a glass of water,
12% said it was to go the toilet,
83% said it was to go home.

Study #3
 The Perfect Breakfast .. . .as a man sees it...

You're sitting at the table and your son is on the cover of the box of Wheaties. Your mistress is on the cover of Playboy. And your wife is on the back of the milk carton.

The Selection Process

A man is dating three women but he can't choose between them. He decides to give them a test. He gives each woman a present of $5,000 and watches to see what they do with the money.

The first does a total makeover. She goes to a fancy beauty salon, gets her hair done, purchases new make-up and buys several new outfits, and dresses up very nicely for the man. She tells him that she has done this to be more attractive for him because she loves him so much. The man was impressed.

The second goes shopping to buy the man gifts. She gets him a new set of golf clubs, some new gizmos for his computer, and some expensive clothes. As she presents these gifts, she tells him that she has spent all the money on him because she loves him so much. Again, the man is impressed.

The third invests the money in the stock market. She earns several times the $5,000. She gives him back his $5000 and reinvests the remainder in a joint account. She tells him that she wants to save for their future because she loves him so much.

Obviously, the he was impressed. The man thought for a long time about what each woman had done with the money, and then he married the one with the largest boobs.

Men are Men.

Bumper Stickers for Ladies

So Many Men, So Few Who Can Afford Me.

God Made Us Sisters, Prozac Made Us Friends.

Coffee, Chocolate, Men ... Some Things Are Just Better Rich.

Don't Treat Me Any Differently than You Would the Queen.

I'm out of Estrogen and I Have a Gun.

Warning: I Have an Attitude and I Know How to Use It.

Of Course I Don't Look Busy...I Did it Right the First Time.

Do Not Start with Me. You Will Not Win.

All Stressed out and No One to Choke.

I Can Be One of Those Bad Things That Happens to Bad People.

How Can I Miss You If You Won't Go Away?
Don't Upset Me! I'm Running out of Places to Hide the Bodies.

If You Want Breakfast in Bed, Sleep in the Kitchen.

How to Maintain Marriage Harmony

Apologies to Henny Youngman
Two times a week, we go to a nice restaurant, have a little wine, some good food and companionship. She goes Tuesdays, I go Fridays.

We also sleep in separate beds. Her's is in Florida and mine is in Toronto.

I take my wife everywhere, but she keeps finding her way back.

I asked my wife where she wanted to go for our anniversary. "Somewhere I haven't been in a long time!" she said. So I suggested the kitchen.

We always hold hands. If I let go, she shops.

She has an electric blender, electric toaster, and, electric bread maker. Then she said, "There are too many gadgets, and no place to sit down!" So I bought her an electric chair.

God created man and rested. Then God created woman. Since then, neither God nor man has rested.

Why do men die before their wives? Because they want to.

Dearly Beloved

A funeral service is being held for a woman who has just passed away. At the end of the service the pall bearers are carrying the casket out when they accidentally bump into a wall, jarring the casket. They hear a faint moan. They open the casket and find that the woman is actually alive!

She lives for ten more years, before she dies. A ceremony is again held at the same funeral home. As the pall bearers are again carrying out the casket, the husband cries out, "Watch the wall!"

Towel Waving 101

An older gentleman marries a younger lady and they are very much in love. However, no matter what the husband does sexually, the woman never achieves orgasm. They decide to ask a marriage counselor.

The counselor listens to their story, and makes the following suggestion. "Hire a strapping young man. While the two of you are making love, have the young man wave a towel over you. That will help the wife fantasize and should bring on an orgasm."
They go home and follow the counselor's advice. They hire a handsome young man and he waves a towel over them as they make love. But, it doesn't help and she is still unsatisfied. Perplexed, they go back to the counselor.

"Okay", says the counselor, "let's try it reversed. Have the young man make love to your wife and you wave the towel over them."

Once again, they follow the advice. The young man gets into bed with the wife and the husband waves the towel. The young man gets to work with great enthusiasm and the wife soon has an enormous, room-shaking, screaming orgasm.

The husband smiles, looks at the young man and says to him triumphantly, "You see, THAT'S the way to wave the towel!"

Same Old Towel - Different Story

A man is getting into the shower, just after his wife finished her shower, when the doorbell rings. After a few seconds of arguing over which one should go and answer the doorbell, the wife gives up, quickly wraps herself up in a towel and runs downstairs.

When she opens the door, there stands Bob, the next door neighbor. Before she says a word, Bob says, "I'll give you $500 to drop that towel that you have on." After thinking for a moment, the woman drops her towel and stands naked in front of Bob.

He admires her for a few seconds, then hands her $500 and leaves.

Confused, but excited about her good fortune, the woman re-wraps herself in the towel and goes back upstairs. When she gets to the bathroom, her husband calls from the shower, "Who was that?"

"It was Bob, the next door neighbor," she replies.

"Great," the husband says. "Did he say anything about the $500 he owes me?"

Math Lesson by Fax

A professor of mathematics sent the following fax to his wife:

"Dear wife,
You must realize that you are 54 years old, and I have certain needs which you are no longer able to satisfy. I am otherwise happy with you as a wife, and sincerely hope you will not be hurt or offended to learn that by the time you receive this fax I will be at the local Red Roof Inn with my 18 year old teaching assistant.

I will be home before midnight,
Your husband

When he arrived at the hotel there was a fax message waiting for him:

Dear Husband,
You too are 54 years old and by the time you receive this fax I will be at the Breakwater Hotel with the 18 year old pool boy. Being the brilliant mathematician that you are, you can easily appreciate the fact that 18 goes into 54 a hell of a lot more times than 54 goes into 18. Don't wait up for me.

Have a nice day!
Your Wife

Seeing Orange

A guy asks a friend, "I have been married to the same woman for 20 years. Is it wrong to think she is sexy?" The friend says "No, I think that's wonderful!"

The guy says, "Every time my wife bends over and I see the curve of her ass, I just have this urge to have sex with her...right there and then!. Well, the other day my wife dropped an orange and she bent. over to pick it up. And that urged hit me and we made mad, passionate love on the spot. Do you think there is anything wrong with that?"

The buddy answers, "Absolutely not. That's great!"

"That's what we thought, but the manger of the Safeway threw us out of the store anyway."

Wrong Answer

A wife asks her husband, "Honey, if I died, would you remarry?"

"After a considerable period of grieving, I guess I would. We all need companionship."

"If I died and you remarried," the wife asks, "would she live in this house?"

"We've spent a lot of money getting this house just the way we want it. I'm not going to sell the house."

"If I died and you remarried, and she lived in this house," the wife asks, "would she sleep in our bed?"

"Well, the bed is brand new, and it cost us $2,000. It's going to last a long time, so I guess she would."

"If I died and you remarried, and she lived in this house and slept in our bed, would she use my golf clubs?"

"Oh, no," the husband replies. "She's left-handed."

Co-Worker Blues

Dave walks into the bar and sees his friend Jeff huddled over the bar, depressed. Dave walks over and asks him what's wrong.

"Well," replies Jeff, "you know that beautiful girl at work that I wanted to ask out, but I got an erection every time I saw her?"

"Yes," replies Dave with a smile.

"Well," says Jeff, straightening up, "I finally plucked up the courage to ask her out, and she agreed."

"That's great!" says Dave, "when are you going out?"

"I went to meet her this evening," continues Jeff, "but I was worried I'd get an erection again. So I got some reinforced packing tape and taped my dick to my leg, so if I did, it wouldn't show."

"Sensible." says Dave.

"So I get to her door," says Jeff, "and I rang her doorbell. And she answered it in the sheerest, tiniest teddy you ever saw."

"And what happened then?"

Jeff huddles over the bar again. "I kicked her in the face."

The Joy of Being a Guy

Car mechanics tell you the truth.
Your last name stays put.
The garage is all yours.
Wedding plans take care of themselves.

Chocolate is just another snack.
You can be president.
You can wear a white T shirt to a water park.
You don't give a damn if someone notices your new haircut.
The world is your urinal.
You never have to drive to another gas station because this one's just too icky.
Same work... more pay.
Wrinkles add character.

Wedding Dress $5000; Tux rental $100.
People never glance at your chest when you're talking to them.
The occasional well-rendered belch is practically expected.
New shoes don't cut, blister, or mangle your feet.
One mood, ALL the time.
 Phone conversations are over in 30 seconds flat.
You know stuff about tanks.
A five-day vacation requires only one suitcase.
You can open all your own jars.
 Dry cleaners and hair cutters don't rob you blind.
You can leave the motel bed unmade.
You get extra credit for the slightest act of thoughtfulness.
If someone forgets to invite you to something, he or she can still be your friend.
Your underwear is $8.95 for a three-pack.
If you are 34 and single, nobody notices.
Everything on your face stays its original color.
You can quietly enjoy a car ride from the passenger's seat.
Three pairs of shoes are more than enough.
You don't have to clean your apartment if the meter reader is coming.
You can quietly watch a game with your buddy for hours without ever thinking: "He must be mad at me."
You don't mooch off other's desserts.
You can drop by to see a friend without having to bring a little gift.
If another guy shows up at the party in the same outfit, you just might become lifelong friends.
You are not expected to know the names of more than five colors.
You don't have to stop and think of which way to turn a nut on a bolt.
You almost never have strap problems in public.
You are unable to see wrinkles in your clothes.
The same hairstyle lasts for years, maybe decades.
You don't have to shave below your neck.
Your belly usually hides your big hips.
One wallet and one pair of shoes, one color, all seasons.
You can "do" your nails with a pocketknife.
You have freedom of choice concerning growing a mustache.
Your pals can be trusted never to trap you with: "So, notice anything different?"
Christmas shopping can be accomplished for 25 relatives, on December 24th in 45 minutes.

About Our Better Halves

Women have strengths that amaze men. They carry children, they carry hardships, they carry burdens, but they hold happiness, love and joy. They smile when they want to scream. They sing when they want to cry. They cry when they are happy and laugh when they are nervous.

Women wait by the phone for a "safe at home call" from a friend after a snowy drive home. They are child care workers, executives, attorneys, stay-at-home moms, biker babes, and your neighbors. They wear suits, jeans, and they wear uniforms. They fight for what they believe in. They stand up to injustice. They walk and talk the extra mile to get their children in the right schools and for getting their family the right health care. They go to the doctor with a frightened friend.

Women are honest, loyal, and forgiving. They are smart, knowing that knowledge is power. But they still know how to use their softer side to make a point. Women want to be the best for their family, their friends, and themselves. Their hearts break when a friend dies. They have sorrow at the loss of a family member, yet they are strong when they think there is no strength left. A woman can make a romantic evening unforgettable.

Women come in all sizes, in all colors and shapes. They live in homes, flats and cabins. They drive, fly, walk, run or E-mail you to show how much they care about you. The heart of a woman is what makes the world spin! Women do more than just give birth. They bring joy and hope. They give compassion and ideals. They give moral support to their family and friends. And all they want back is a hug, a smile and for you to do the same to people you come in contact with.

Men are good at lifting heavy stuff.

The Widow

A lonely widow, Zelda. was sitting on a beach in Florida, attempting to strike up a conversation with the older gentleman reading a book on the next lounge chair.

"Hello, sir," she chirped, "do you like movies?" *"Yes, I do,"* he responded, then returned to his book.

Zelda persisted. "Do you like gardening?" The man again looked up from his book. *"Yes, I do,"* he informed her politely before returning to his reading.

Undaunted, Zelda continued., "Do you like pussycats?" With that, the man dropped his book and pounced on her, ravishing her as she'd never been ravished before. As the cloud of sand around them began to settle, Zelda asked the man, "How did you know that's what I wanted?" He replied, *"How did you know my name was Katz?"*

Union Benefits

A dedicated union worker was attending a convention in Las Vegas and, as you would expect, he decided to check out the local brothels nearby. When he got to the first one, he asked the madam, "Is this a union house?"

"No," she replied, "I'm sorry it isn't."

"Well, if I pay you $100, what cut do the girls get?"

"The house gets $80 and the girls get $20."

Mightily offended at such unfair dealings, the man stomped off down the street in search of a more equitable, hopefully unionized shop.

His search continued until finally he reached a brothel where the Madame responded,

"Why yes sir, this IS a union house."

The man asked, "And if I pay you $100, what cut do the girls get?"
"The girls get $80 and the house gets $20."

"That's more like it!" the man said. He looked around the room and pointed to a stunningly attractive blonde. "I'd like her for the night."

"I'm sure you would, sir," said the Madame, then, gesturing to an obese fifty-five year old woman in the corner, "but Ethel here has seniority."

The Nudist Colony

Bob joins a very exclusive nudist colony. On his first day he takes off his clothes and starts wandering around.

A gorgeous petite blonde walks by him and the man immediately gets an erection. The woman notices his erection, comes over to him grinning sweetly and says: "Sir, did you call for me?"

Bob replies: "No. What do you mean?"

She says: "You must be new here. Let me explain. It's a rule here that if I give you an erection, it implies you called for me." Smiling, she then leads him to the side of a pool, lays down on a towel, eagerly pulls him to her and happily lets him have his way with her.

Bob continues exploring the facilities. He enters a steam room, sits down, and farts. Within a few seconds a huge, horribly corpulent, hairy man with a firm erection lumbers out of the steam towards him.

The huge man says: "Sir, did you call for me?"

Bob replies: "No. What do you mean?"

"You must be new here; it is a rule that when you fart, it implies you called for me."

The huge man then easily spins Bob around, bends him over the bench and has his way with him.

Bob rushes back to the colony office. He is greeted by the smiling naked receptionist: "May I help you?"

Bob says: "Here is your card and key back. You can keep the $500 joining fee."

Receptionist: "But Sir, you've only been here a couple of hours; you only saw a small fraction of our facilities.....

Bob replies: "Listen lady, I am 58 years old. I get a hard-on once a month, but I fart 15 times a day!"

Restaurant Buzz

A man goes into a restaurant, sits down at a table and examines the menu. When the waitress asks for his order, says, "I want a quickie."

She slaps his face and asks, "Now would you please give me your order?"

Again, he says, "I want a quickie."

She slaps him again and says, "I'll give you one last chance; what do you want?"

Someone from the next table leans over and says quietly to the man, "I think it's pronounced QUICHE."

Love Train

A man and a woman who have never met before find themselves assigned to the same sleeping room on a transcontinental train. They called over a conductor who informed them that there were no other sleeping cabins available. Their only other options was to sit in a riding car. After the initial embarrassment and uneasiness, they both said they needed to sleep.

They took turns changing clothes in the little bathroom. The man climbed into the upper berth, and the woman in the lower berth.

In the middle of the night the man leans over, wakes the woman and says, "I'm sorry to bother you, but I'm awfully cold and I was wondering if you could possibly reach over and get me another blanket?

The woman leans out and, with a glint in her eye, says, "I have a better idea. Just for tonight let's pretend that we are married."

The man happily replies, "OK. Awesome!"

The woman says "GOOD.... Get your own fucking blanket."

Technique

Two married buddies are out drinking one night when one turns to the other and says, "You know, I don't know what else to do. Whenever I go home after we've been out drinking, I turn the headlights off before I get to the driveway. I shut off the engine and coast into the garage. I take my shoes off before I go into the house, I sneak up the stairs. I get undressed in the bathroom. I ease into bed and my wife STILL wakes up and yells at me for staying out so late!"

His buddy looks at him and says, "Well, you're obviously taking the wrong approach. I screech into the driveway, slam the door, storm up the steps, throw my shoes into the closet, jump into bed, slap her on the butt and say, 'You as horny as I am?' . . . and, she's always sound asleep!"

Curled

Bert met Flo in a bar one night and began buying her drinks. They hit it off pretty well, and soon Bert suggested that they go to his apartment for some extracurricular activity. It wasn't long before they found themselves in bed making passionate love. As they were making love, though, Bert noticed that Flo's toes would curl up as he was thrusting in and out.

When they were done, Bert laid back on the bed and said, "I must have been pretty good tonight. I noticed your toes curling up when I was going in and out."

Flo looked at him and smiled. "That usually happens when someone forgets to remove my pantyhose.

The Sandals

This married couple were on holiday in Morocco. They were touring around the marketplace looking at the goods and such when they passed this small sandal shop.

From inside they heard a gentlemen with a Moroccan accent say, "You foreigners, come in. Come into my humble shop".

Curious, the married couple entered.

The Moroccan man said to them. "I have some special sandals I tink you would be interested in. Dey make you wild at sex like a great desert camel."

The wife was really interested in buying the sandals after what the shop owner said, but her husband felt he really didn't need them, being the sex god he was.

The husband asked the man, "How could sandals make you into a sex freak?"

The Moroccan replied, "Just try dem on, Saiheeb."

Well, the husband, after much badgering from his wife, finally conceded to try them on. As soon as he slipped them onto his feet, he got this wild look in his eyes; something his wife hadn't seen in many years - raw sexual power.

In a blink of an eye, the husband grabbed the Moroccan man, bent him violently over a table, yanked down his pants, and grabbed a firm hold of the Moroccan's thighs.

The Moroccan then began screaming. "YOU HAVE DEM ON DE WRONG FEET!"

The Poker Guys

Six Jewish gentlemen were playing poker in the condo clubhouse when Meyerowitz loses $500 on a single hand, clutches his chest and drops dead at the table.

Showing respect for their fallen comrade, the other five complete their playing time standing up.
Finkelstein looks around and asks "Now, who is going to tell the wife?"

They draw straws. Goldberg, who is always a loser, picks the short one. They tell him to be discreet, be gentle, don't make a bad situation any worse than it is.

"Gentlemen! Discreet? I'm the most discreet mensch you will ever meet. Discretion is my middle name, leave it to me."

Goldberg goes over to the Meyerowitz apartment, knocks on the door, When the wife answers, and asks what he wants.

Goldberg declares "Your husband just lost $500 playing cards."

She hollers, "TELL HIM HE SHOULD DROP DEAD!"

Goldberg says, "Okay, I'll tell him."

Sex on the Sabbath

A man wonders if having sex on the Sabbath is a sin because he is not sure if sex is work or play. So he goes to a priest and asks for his opinion on this question.

After consulting the Bible, the priest says, "My son, after an exhaustive search, I am positive that sex is work and is therefore not permitted on Sundays."

The man thinks: "What does a priest know about sex?" So he goes to a minister, who after all is a married man and experienced in this matter.

He queries the minister and receives the same reply. Sex is work and therefore not for the Sabbath!

Not pleased with the reply, he seeks out the ultimate authority: A man with thousands of years tradition and knowledge. In other words, he goes to a rabbi. The rabbi ponders the question, then states, " Sex is definitely not work!"

The man replies, "Rabbi, how can you be so sure when the other clergymen I talked with tell me sex is work?"

The rabbi softly speaks, "If sex were work, my wife would have the maid do it."

Love Styles of the Non-Rich and Ordinary

Three men are discussing their previous night's lovemaking.

The Italian says, "My wife, I rubbed her all over with fine olive oil, then we make wonderful love. She screamed for five minutes."

The Frenchman says, "I smooth sweet butter on my wife's body, then we made passionate love.
She screamed for 20 minutes."

The Jewish guy says, "I covered my wife's body with schmaltz (chicken fat). We made love and she screamed for six hours."

The others say, "SIX HOURS? How did you make her scream for six hours?"

He shrugs. "I wiped my hands on the drapes."

Ke Moh Saby

A man boards an airplane and as soon as he's seated, he glances up and sees a most beautiful woman boarding the plane. He soon realizes she is heading straight towards his seat. A wave of nervous anticipation washes over him.

Lo and behold, she takes the seat right beside his. Eager to strike up a conversation, he blurts out, "Business trip or vacation?"

She turns, smiles and says, "Business. I'm going to the annual Nymphomaniac Convention in Chicago."

Whoa!!! He swallows hard and is instantly crazed with excitement. Here's the most gorgeous woman he has ever seen, sitting right next to him and she's going to a meeting of nymphomaniacs!

Struggling to maintain his outward cool, he calmly asks, "What's your business role at this convention?"

She says, "Lecturer. I use my experiences to debunk some of the popular myths about sexuality."

"Really," he says, swallowing hard, "what myths are those?"

"Well," she explains, "one popular myth is that African American men are the most well-endowed when, in fact, it is the Native American Indian who is most likely to possess that trait. Another popular myth is that French men are the best lovers, when actually it is men of Jewish descent."

Suddenly, the woman becomes very embarrassed and blushes. "I'm sorry," she says, "I shouldn't be discussing this with you, I don't even know your name!"

"Tonto. Tonto Rubinstein."

A Woman's Fantasy

Most experts agree that most common fantasy women have is having two men at once. While this has been verified by a several recent sociological studies, it appears that most men do not realize that in this fantasy, one man is cooking and the other is cleaning.

The Newlyweds

A young couple were married, and celebrated their first night together, doing what newlyweds do, time and time again, all night long.

When they get up in the morning, the groom goes into the bathroom but finds no towel when he emerges from the shower. He asks the bride to please bring one from the bedroom.

When she gets to the bathroom door, he opened the door, exposing his body for the first time in the light to his bride where she sees all of him well.

Her eyes went up and down and at about midway, her eyes stopped and stared, and she asked shyly, "What's that?" pointing to a small part of his anatomy.

He, also being shy, thought for a minute and then said, "Well, that's what we had so much fun with last night."

And she, in amazement, asked, "Is that all we have left?"

The Chicken Farmer

While the bar patron savored a double martini, an attractive woman sat down next to him. The bartender served her a glass of orange juice, and the man turned to her and said, "This is a special day. I'm celebrating."

"I'm celebrating, too," she replied, clinking glasses with him.

"What are you celebrating?"

"For years I've been trying to have a child," she answered, "today, my gynecologist told me I'm pregnant!"

"Congratulations," the man said, lifting his glass. "As it happens, I'm a chicken farmer, and for years all my hens were infertile. But today they're finally fertile."

"How did it happen?"

"I switched cocks."

"What a coincidence," she said, smiling "That's exactly what I did!"

The Eternal Question

A chicken and an egg are lying in bed. The chicken is leaning against the headboard smoking a cigarette with a satisfied smile on its face.

The egg, looking a ticked off, grabs the sheet and rolls over and says, "Well, I guess we finally answered THAT question!"

New?

A guy out on the golf course takes a high speed ball right in the crotch.

Writhing in agony, he falls to the ground. He finally gets himself to the doctor. He says, "How bad is it doc? I'm going on my honeymoon next week and my bride to be is still a virgin in every way."

The doc said , "I'll have to put your unit in a splint to let it heal and keep it straight. It should be okay next week."

So the sawbones took four tongue depressors and formed a neat little 4-sided bandage and wired it all together. It was an impressive work of art.

The guy mentions none of this to his girlfriend. They marry and on their honeymoon night in the hotel room, she rips open her blouse to reveal a gorgeous set of boobs. This was the first time he ever saw them.

She says: "You are the first, no one has ever touched these breasts."

He pulls down his pants, whips it out and says,...

"Look at this. It's still in the crate!"

Section Ten: Lawyers!

With apologies to my daughter and daughter-in-law!

Law at the Bar

A man walks into a bar. He sees a beautiful, well-dressed woman sitting on a bar stool alone.

He walks up to her and says, "Hi there, how's it going tonight?"

She turns to him, looks him straight in the eyes and says, "I'll screw anybody at any time, any where -- your place or my place, it doesn't matter to me."

The guy raises his eyebrows and says... "Really, what law firm do you work for?"

A Quarter for Your Thoughts

A dad walks into a Mall followed by his ten-year-old son. The kid is flipping a 25 cent piece in the air and catching it between his teeth.

As they walk through the Mall, someone bumps into the boy at just the wrong moment and the coin goes straight into his mouth and lodges in his throat. He immediately starts choking, and turning blue in the face. His fater panics and starts shouting for help.

A well dressed middle-aged, attractive but serious looking woman is sitting at a coffee bar in the food court of the Mall reading her newspaper and sipping a cup of coffee. At the sound of the commotion, she looks up, puts her coffee cup down, neatly folds her newspaper and places it on the counter.

She makes her unhurried way across the Mall to the choking youngster. Reaching the boy, the woman carefully takes hold of the boy's testicles and squeezes gently at first and then ever more firmly. After a few seconds, the boy convulses violently and coughs up the quarter. The woman deftly catches the coin in her free hand. Releasing the boy, the woman hands the coin to the father and walks back to her seat in the coffee bar without saying a word. As soon as he is sure that his son has suffered no lasting ill-effects, the father rushes over to the woman and starts effusively thanking her saying, "I've never seen anybody do anything like that before--it was fantastic, doctor!"

"Heavens, no," the woman replies, "I'm not a doctor. I'm a Divorce Attorney."

Counselor, is it True...

1. Did you hear about the new sushi bar that caters exclusively to lawyers?
It's called, Sosumi.

2. Did you hear that the Post Office just recalled their latest stamps?
They had pictures of lawyers on them...and people couldn't figure out which side to spit on.

3. How are an apple and a lawyer alike?
They both look good hanging from a tree.

4. How can a pregnant woman tell that she's carrying a future lawyer?
She has an uncontrollable craving for bologna.

5. How does an attorney sleep?
First he lies on one side, then he lies on the other.

6. How many lawyer jokes are there?
Only three. The rest are true stories.

7. How many lawyers does it take to screw in a light bulb?
Three, one to climb the ladder. One to shake it. And one to sue the ladder company.

8. If a lawyer and an IRS agent were both drowning, and you could only save one of them, would you go to lunch or read your newspaper?

9. What are lawyers good for?
They make used car salesmen look good.

10. What did the terrorist that hijacked a jumbo-jet full of lawyers do?
He threatened to release one every hour if his demands were not met.

11. What do dinosaurs and decent lawyers have in common?
They are both extinct.

12. What do lawyers and sperm have in common?
It takes 300,000 of them to make one human being.

13. What do you call 25 attorneys buried up to their chins in cement?
Not enough cement.

14. What do you call 25 skydiving lawyers?
A round of Skeet.

15. What do you call a lawyer gone bad?
Senator.

16. What do you call a lawyer with an IQ of 50?
Your Honor

17. What do you throw to a drowning lawyer?
His partners.

18. What does a lawyer do after sex?
Pays the bill.

19. What does a lawyer get when you give him Viagra?
Taller.

20. What's brown and looks really good on a lawyer?
A Doberman.

20. What is the difference between a lawyer and a liar?
The pronunciation.

21. What's the difference between a lawyer and a prostitute?
The prostitute stops screwing you after you are dead.

22. What's the difference between a lawyer and a vulture?
The lawyer gets frequent flyer miles.

23. What's the difference between a mosquito and a lawyer?
One is a bloodsucking parasite, the other is an insect.

24. Where can you find a good lawyer?
The nearest cemetery.

25. Why did God make snakes just before lawyers?
To practice.

26. Why does California have the most lawyers in the country, and New Jersey have the most toxic waste sites?
New Jersey got first choice.

Bessie

Clyde, a farmer, was suing a big trucking company for an accident caused when a tractor-trailer smashed into his truck. The attorney for the trucking company tried to rattle Clyde and his story.

Attorney: "Now, Clyde, what did you tell the State Trooper when he arrived at the scene of the accident?"

Clyde: "Well, my mule, Bessie, was riding in my trailer hitch when this big tractor trailer..."

Attorney: "Stop right there Clyde. Now, you tell the judge exactly what you told the State Trooper when he arrived at the scene of the accident?"

Clyde: "Well, now it was like this... my mule Bessie was in the hitch behind my truck when this big tractor trailer came..."

Attorney: "Hold on now Clyde. Did you or did you not tell the State Trooper, when he arrived at the scene, 'I'm feelin' fine'?"

Clyde: "Now my mule Bessie was in the hitch behind the truck when this big tractor trailer..."

Attorney: "Now, Clyde, I want a **yes** or **no**. Did you or did you not tell the State Trooper when he arrived at the scene, 'I'm feelin' fine'?!!"

Clyde: "Yes, but..."

Attorney: "That's all I wanted hear! Judge, I demand that this case be thrown out of court. This man is attempting to perpetrate a fraud against my client!"

Judge: "Counselor, now you hold on. I want to hear what this man has to say. Clyde, you go on and tell me exactly what happened."

Clyde: "Well, your honor. I was going over to friend's farm to help him clear a field of tree stumps and rocks. I loaded my mule Bessie into my trailer hitch. We was riding down the highway, keepin' to the speed limit, mind you, when this big tractor-trailer came right through a stop sign with barely a pause and smashed right into the side of my truck.

Well, the impact sent me into a ditch on one side of the road and poor Bessie to the other side. I'm lying on ground hurtin' pretty bad. My leg was broke. My ribs was broke. My body was bruised all up.

Bessie, on the other side of the road was hurtin' too. She was makin' a huge ruckus...hee-hawing, and braying, and carrying on somethin' awful.

Well, the State Trooper comes on the scene and he sees old Bessie just carrying on makin' all that ruckus. He pulls out this big gun and shoots my Bessie right in the head!"

Then he comes over to me carrying that big gun of his and says, 'How you feelin?'"

Section Eleven: The Clinton Years

Before there was Clinton in the White House, there was a Clinton in New York ... (oh, yes, and a hotel).

The First Visit by the New President

George W. Bush was invited to a high level meeting at the White House shortly after the election was decided. After drinking several glasses of iced tea, he asked Bill Clinton if he could use his personal bathroom.

He was astonished to see that the President had a solid gold urinal. That afternoon, George told his wife, Laura, about the urinal. "Just think," he said," when I am President, I'll get to have a gold urinal!"

The next day, when Laura had lunch with Hillary, she told Hillary how impressed George had been with his discovery of the gold urinal in the President's private bathroom.

That evening, Bill and Hillary were getting ready for bed. Hillary turned to Bill and said, "Well, I found out who peed in your saxophone."

The Call

Saddam Hussein called President Clinton and said, "Bill, I had a wonderful dream last night. I could see America, the whole country, and on each house I saw a banner."

"What did it say on the banners?" Mr. Clinton asked. Saddam replied, "LONG LIVE SADDAM HUSSEIN."

Mr. Clinton responded, "You know, Saddam, I am really happy you called. Last night I had a similar dream. I could see all of Baghdad, and it was more beautiful than ever. It had been rebuilt completely, and on each house flew an enormous banner."

"What did the banners say?" Saddam asked.

"I don't know," replied President Clinton, "I can't read Hebrew."

The Option

Clinton dies and goes straight to hell. When he arrives the Devil greets him and offers him three ways to spend eternity. They go to the first door and the Devil shows him Newt Gingrich, hanging from the ceiling with fire under him. Bill says "Oh no! That's not how I want to spend all eternity."

They go to the second door. The Devil shows him Rush Limbaugh chained to the wall being tortured. Bill says "Oh no! Not for me!"

They go to the third door. Behind it is Ken Starr, chained to the wall with Monica Lewinsky on her knees giving him a blow job. Bill thinks and decides, "Hmmm, looks okay to me. I'll take it."

The Devil then says, "Good! Hey, Monica, you've been replaced."

I'm Next

An airplane was about to crash, and there were 5 passengers left, but only 4 parachutes. The first passenger, Bill Clinton said, "I am President of the United States, and I have a great responsibility, being the leader of nearly 300 million people, and a superpower, etc."

So he takes the first parachute, and jumps out of the plane.

The second passenger, said,"I'm Gary Sheffield, the greatest baseball player in the world, so I can't afford to die." So he takes the second parachute, and leaves the plane.

The third passenger, Hillary Clinton, said "I am the wife of the President of the United States, a soon to be New York Senator, and I am the smartest woman in the world." So she
 takes the third parachute and exits the plane.

The fourth passenger, Pope John Paul II, says to the fifth passenger, a 10 year old boy scout, "I am old and frail and I don't have many years left. As a Christian gesture and a good deed, I will sacrifice my life and let you have the last parachute."

The boy scout said, "It's Ok, there's a parachute for both of us. The world's smartest woman took my backpack."

Stuff Conservative Republicans

Love

One of the nation's largest soup manufacturers announced today that they will be stocking America's shelves this week with their newest soup creation, "Clinton Soup", that will honor one of the nation's former presidents. It consists primarily of a small weenie in hot water.

Chrysler Corporation is adding a new car to its line to honor Bill Clinton. The Dodge Drafter will begin production in Canada this year.

When Clinton was asked what he thought about foreign affairs, he replied:
"I don't know, I never had one."

If you came across Bill Clinton struggling in a raging river and you had a choice between rescuing him or getting a Pulitzer Prize-winning photograph, what shutter speed would you use?

Chelsea asked her dad, "Do all fairy tales begin with once upon a time?"
Bill Clinton replied, "No, some begin with 'After I'm elected'."

Clinton's mother prayed fervently that Bill would grow up and be President of the United States..
Half of her prayer was been answered.

American Indians have nicknamed Bill Clinton as "Walking Eagle" because he is so full of crap he can't fly.

Clinton only lacks three things to become known as one of America's finest leaders: integrity, vision, and wisdom.

Clinton is doing the work of three men: Larry, Curly, and Mo.

Revised judicial oath: "I solemnly swear to tell the truth as I know it, the whole truth as I believe it to be, and nothing but what I think you need to know."

Politicians and diapers have one thing in common. They should both be changed regularly, and for the same reason.

Section Twelve: Politically Incorrect

My mother used to say that if you can't say something nice about somebody say something that will really tick them off!

Sermon

A new priest at his first mass was so nervous he could hardly speak. After mass, he asked the monsignor how he had done. The monsignor replied, "When I am worried about getting nervous on the pulpit, I put a glass of vodka next to the water pitcher. If I start to get nervous, I take a sip of the vodka. The vodka is clear and the parishioners will think you are drinking water

The next Sunday he took the monsignor's advice. At the beginning of the sermon, he got nervous and took a drink and another and another. He proceeded to talk up a storm.

Upon his return to his office after mass, he found the following note on the door:

1. Sip the vodka, don't gulp.
2. There are 10 commandments, not 12.
3. There are 12 disciples, not 10.
4. Jesus was consecrated, not constipated.
5. Jacob wagered his donkey. He did not bet his ass.
6. We do not refer to Jesus Christ as the late J. C.
7. The Father, Son, and Holy Ghost are not referred to as Daddy, Junior and the Spook.
8. David slew Goliath, he did not kick the shit out of him.
9. When David was hit by a rock and was knocked off his donkey, don't say he was stoned off his ass.
10. We do not refer to the cross as the "Big T.
11. When Jesus broke the bread at the Last Supper he said, "Take this and eat it for it is my body." He did not say "Eat me"
12. The Virgin Mary is not called "Mary with the Cherry."
13. The recommended grace before a meal is not: Rub-A-Dub-Dub thanks for the grub, yeah, God!
14. Next Sunday there will be a taffy pulling contest at St. Peter's. not a peter pulling contest at St. Taffy's.

The Luck of the Irish

Two men were sitting next to each other at a bar. After a while, one guy looks at the other and says, "I can't help but think, from listening to you, that you're from Ireland. The other guy responds proudly, "Yes, that I am!"

The first guy says, "So am I! And where about from Ireland might you be?"

The other guy answers, "I'm from Dublin, I am."

The first guy responds, "Sure and begora, and so am I! And what street did you live on in Dublin?"

The other guy says, "A lovely little area it was. I lived on McCleary Street in the old central part of town."

The first guy says, "Faith, and it's a small world, so did I! And to what school would you have been going?"

The other guy answers, "Well now, I went to St.Mary's."

The first guy gets really excited, and says, "And so did I. And tell me, what year did you graduate?"

The other guy answers, "Well, now, I graduated in 1964."

The first guy exclaims, "The Good Lord must be smiling down upon us! I can hardly believe our good luck at winding up in the same bar on this very night. Can you believe it, I graduated from St. Mary's in 1964 my own self!"

About this time, another guy walks into the bar, sits down, and orders a beer. The bartender walks over shaking his head and mutters, "It's going to be a long night tonight, the Murphy twins are drunk again."

Saints Preserve Us

The bartender was washing his glasses, when an elderly Irishman came in. With great difficulty, the Irishman hoisted his bad leg over the barstool, pulled himself up painfully, and asked for a sip of Irish whiskey. The Irishman looked down the bar and said, "Is that Jesus down there?" The bartender nodded yes. The Irishman told him to give Jesus an Irish whiskey, too.

The next patron to come in was an ailing Italian with a hunched back, who moved very slowly. He shuffled up to the barstool and asked for a glass of Chianti. He also looked down the bar and asked if that was Jesus sitting at the end f the bar. The bartender nodded, so the Italian said to give him a glass of Chianti, too.

The third patron to enter the bar was a redneck, who swaggered into the bar and hollered, "Barkeeper, set me up a cold one! Hey, is that God's boy down there?" The barkeeper nodded. The redneck told him to give Jesus a cold one, too.

As Jesus got up to leave, he walked over to the Irishman and touched him and said, "For your kindness, you are healed!" The Irishman felt the strength come back to his leg, so he got up and danced a jig out the door. Jesus touched the Italian and said, "For your kindness, you are healed!" The Italian felt his back straighten, so he raised his hands above his head and did a flip out the door.

Jesus walked toward the redneck, but the redneck jumped back and exclaimed, "Don't touch me! I'm drawin' disability!"

"Irish Prayer"

Murphy was staggering home with a pint of booze in his back pocket when he slipped and fell heavily. Struggling to his feet, he felt something wet running down his leg.

"Please Lord", he implored, "let it be blood!!"

"Irish Shopping"

McQuillan walked into a bar and ordered martini after martini, each time removing the olives and placing them in a jar. When the jar was filled with olives and all the drinks consumed, the Irishman started to leave.

"S' cuse me", said a customer, who was puzzled over what McQuillan had done, "what was that all about?"

"Nothin', said the Irishman, "my wife just sent me out for a jar of olives!"

"You've Been Out Drinking Again"

An Irishman had been drinking at a pub all night. The bartender finally said that the bar is closing. So the Irishman stood up to leave fell flat on his face. He tried to stand one more time; same result. He figured he'll crawl outside and get some fresh air and maybe that will sober him up. Once outside, he stood up and fell on his face again.

He decided to crawl the four blocks home. When he arrived at the door he stood up and fell flat on his face. He crawled through the door and into his bedroom. When he reached his bed he tried one more time to stand up. This time he managed to pull himself upright, but he quickly fell right into the bed and is sound asleep as soon as his head hit the pillow.

He was awakened the next morning to his wife standing over him, shouting, "SO YOU'VE BEEN DRINKING AGAIN!" Putting on an innocent look, and intent on bluffing it out he said, "What makes you say that?"

"The pub just called; you left your wheelchair there again."

"I've Lost Me Luggage"

An Irishman arrived at J.F.K. Airport and wandered around the terminal with tears streaming down his cheeks. An airline employee asked him if he was already homesick. "No," replied the Irishman. "I've lost all me luggage!" "How'd that happen?"

"The cork fell out!" said the Irishman.

"Water to Wine"

An Irish priest is driving down to New York and gets stopped for speeding in Connecticut. The state trooper smells alcohol on the priest's breath and then sees an empty wine bottle on the floor of the car.

The trooper says, "Sir, have you been drinking?"

"Just water," says the priest. The trooper says, "Then why do I smell wine?"

The priest looks at the bottle and says, "Good Lord! He's done it again!"

"The Brothel"

Two Irishmen were sitting a pub having beer and watching the brothel across the street. They saw a Baptist minister walk into the brothel, and one of them said, "Aye, 'tis a shame to see a man of the cloth goin' bad."

Then they saw a rabbi enter the brothel, and the other Irishman said, "Aye, 'tis a shame to see that the Jews are fallin' victim to temptation."

Then they saw a Catholic priest enter the brothel, and one of the Irishmen said, "What a terrible pity... one of the girls must be quite ill."

"Lost at Sea"

Two Irishmen, Patrick & Michael, were adrift in a lifeboat following a dramatic escape from a burning freighter. While rummaging through the boat's provisions, Patrick stumbled across an old lamp. Secretly hoping that a genie would appear, he rubbed the lamp vigorously. To the amazement of Patrick, a genie came forth.

This particular genie, however, stated that he could only deliver one wish, not the usual three. Without giving much thought to the matter, Patrick blurted out, "Make the entire ocean into Guinness!"

The genie clapped his hands with a deafening crash, and immediately the entire sea turned into the finest brew ever sampled by mortals. Simultaneously, the genie vanished.

Only the gentle lapping of Guinness on the hull broke the stillness as the two men considered their circumstances. Michael looked disgustedly at Patrick whose wish had been granted. After a long, tension-filled moment, he spoke: "Nice going Patrick! Now we're going to have to pee in the boat."

Sainthood

Brothers Mike and Seamus O'Malley were the two richest men in town and both were complete scoundrels. They swindled the Church out of its property, foreclosed on the orphanage, and cheated widows out of their income. And that was just for starters.

When Seamus dies, Mike pays a visit to the priest. "Father," he says, "my good name will be upheld in this town. You'll be givin' the eulogy for me brother, and in that eulogy you are going to say "Seamus O'Malley was truly a saint."

The priest said "I won't do such a thing. T'would be a lie!"

"I know you will," says Mike. "I hold the mortgage on the parish school, and if you don't say those words, I'll foreclose." The priest is over a barrel. "And if I pledge to say those words, then you'll sign the note over free and clear?" "Done," cackles Mike, and he signs over the note. Next morning at the funeral, the priest begins the eulogy: "Seamus O'Malley was a mean-spirited, spiteful, penurious, lying, cheating, arrogant and hateful excuse for a human being. But compared to his brother, Mike, Seamus O'Malley was truly a saint!"

Confession

The new nun goes to her first confession. She tells the priest that she has a terrible secret and he tells her that her secret is safe in the sanctity of the confessional.

She says, "Father, I never wear panties under my habit."

The priest chuckles and says, "That's not so serious. Say five Hail Marys, five Our Fathers and do six cartwheels on your way to the altar."

Polish Air Disaster

Poland's worst air disaster occurred today when a small two-seater Cessna 152 plane crashed into a cemetery early this afternoon in central Poland.

Polish search and rescue workers have recovered 826 bodies so far and expect that number to climb as digging continues into the evening

Polish Lunch

An Irishman, a Mexican and a Pole were doing construction work on scaffolding on the 20th floor of a building.

They were eating lunch and the Irishman said: "Corned beef and cabbage! If I get corned beef and cabbage one more time for lunch I'm going to jump off this building."

The Mexican opened his lunch box and exclaimed, "Burritos again! If I get burritos one more time I'm going to jump off too."

The Pole opened his lunch and said, "Bologna again. If I get a bologna sandwich one more time I'm jumping too."

Next day the Irishman opens his lunch box, sees corned beef and cabbage and jumps to his death.

The Mexican opens his lunch, sees a burrito and jumps too.

The Pole opens his lunch, sees the bologna sandwich and jumps to his death also.

At the funeral, the Irishman's wife is weeping. She says, "If I'd known how really tired he was of corned beef and cabbage I never would have given it to him again!"

The Mexican's wife also weeps and says, "I could have given him tacos or enchiladas! I didn't realize he hated burritos so much."

The ladies turned and to the Pole's wife. "Hey, don't look at me," she said. "He made his own lunch."

Some Hot Dog

A man goes into the store and tells the clerk, "I'd like some Polish sausage."

The clerk looks at him and says, "Are you Polish?"

The guy, clearly offended, says, "Well, yes I am. But let me ask you if I had asked for Italian sausage, would you ask me if I was Italian? Or if I had asked for Bratwurst would you ask me if I was German? If I had ordered a kosher hot dog would you have asked me if I was Jewish? Or if I had asked for taco, would you ask if I was Mexican? Huh? Would ya??"

The clerk says, "Well, no."

With deep self righteous indignation, the guy says, "Well, all right then, why did you ask me if I'm Polish just because I ask for Polish sausage?

The clerk says, "Because this is a hardware store."

Who's in Charge

An Italian, a Scotsman and a Chinese fellow are hired at a construction site. The foreman points out a huge pile of sand and says to the Italian guy, "You're in charge of sweeping."

To the Scotsman he says, "You're in charge of shoveling."

And to the Chinese guy, "You're in charge of supplies."

He then says, "Now, I have to leave for a little while. I expect you guys to make a dent in that there pile."

The foreman goes away for a couple hours and when he returns, the pile of sand is untouched.

He asks the Italian, "Why didn't you sweep any of it?" The Italian replies, "I no hava no broom. You saida to the Chinese a fella that he a wasa in a charge of supplies, but he hasa disappeared and I no coulda finda him nowhere."

Then the foreman turns to the Scotsman and says, And you, I thought I told you to shovel this pile."

The Scotsman replies, "Aye, ye did lad, boot ah couldnay get me self a shoovel! Ye left th' Chinese gadgie in chairge of supplies, boot ah couldnay fin' him either."

The foreman is really angry now and storms off toward the pile of sand to look for the Chinese guy ... Just then, the Chinese guy leaps out from behind the pile of sand and yells

SUPPLIES!!

Gator-Aide

A stock broker in Georgia decided that he wanted to throw a party and invited all of his buddies and neighbors. He also invited Leroy, his black chauffeur to enjoy the fun. The party was held around the pool in the backyard of the lawyer's mansion.

Everyone was having a good time drinking, dancing, eating shrimp, oysters and BBQ. At the height of the party, the stock broker said, "I have a ten foot, man-eating gator in my pool and I'll give a million dollars to anyone who has the guts to jump in."

The words were barely out of the stock broker's mouth when there was a loud splash and everyone turned around and saw Leroy in the pool! Leroy was fighting the gator and kicking its ass! Leroy was jabbing the gator in the eyes with his thumbs, throwing punches, doing all kinds of stuff like head butts and choke holds, biting the gator on the tail and flipping the gator through the air like some kind of Japanese Judo instructor.

The water was churning and splashing everywhere. Both Leroy and the gator were screaming and raising hell. Finally, Leroy strangled the gator and let it sink to the bottom like a carnival goldfish.

Leroy slowly climbed out of the pool. Everybody was just staring at him in disbelief. Finally, the stock broker says, "Well, Leroy, I reckon I owe you a million dollars."

"No, that's okay. I don't want it," said Leroy.

The stock broker insisted. "Man, I have to give you something. You won the bet. How about half a million bucks then?"

"No thanks. I don't want it," answered Leroy.

The stock broker said, "Come on, I insist on giving you something. That was amazing. How about a new Porsche and a Rolex and some stock options?"

Still, the brother said no.

The confused stock broker said, "Well, Leroy, then what do you want?"

Leroy said, "I want the name of the son of a bitch who pushed me into the pool..."

Small Wonder

This guy owns a horse stud farm, and gets a call from a friend. "I know this midget with a speech impediment who wants to buy a horse. I'm sending him over."

Midget arrives, and the owner asks if he wants a male or female horse.

"A female horth," the midget replies.

So the owner shows him one.

"Nith looking horth, can I see her mouth?"

So the owner picks up the midget and shows him the horse's mouth.

"Nith mouth. Can I see her eyesth?"

The owner picks up the midget to eye level.

"Ok, what about the earsth?"

Now the owner is getting pissed, but he picks up the midget one more time and shows the ears.

"OK, finally, I'd like to see her twat."

With that, the owner picks up the midget and shoves his head up the horse's twat, then pulls him out.

Shaking his head, the midget says, "Perhapth I should rephrase that. I'd like to see her run..

Section: Thirteen: Yiddish You Don't Have to Know

Jewish you don't have to be....

The Hebrew Cave Drawings

A team of archaeologists was excavating in Israel when they came upon a cave. Written on the wall of the cave were the following symbols in order of appearance:

1. A woman
2. A donkey
3. A shovel
4. A fish
5. A Star of David

They decided that this was a unique find and the writings were at least more than three thousand years old. They photographed the drawings, enlarged the photos and displayed at a museum. Archaeologists from all over the world were invited to study the ancient symbols.

The scholars held meetings and more meetings to contemplate the cave drawings. After months of conferences and discussions, these leading world experts came to a consensus as to the meanings of the markings.

The public was invited to hear what these learned men had concluded. The photograph, enlarged to mural size, were placed on a stage of a large auditorium in Jerusalem. The President of the Archaeological Society stood up and pointed at the first drawing and said, "This looks like a woman. We can judge that this tribe was family oriented and held women in high esteem. You can also tell they were intelligent, as the next symbol resembles a donkey, indicating they were smart enough to use animals to till the soil. The next drawing looks like a shovel of some sort, which means they used tools as well. Even further proof of their high intelligence is the fish which means that if a famine hit the earth, whereby the food didn't grow, they would take to the sea for food. The last symbol appears to be the Star of David which means they were evidently Hebrews."

The audience applauded enthusiastically and the President smiled and said, "I'm glad to see that you are all in full agreement with our interpretations."

Suddenly a little old man stood up in the back of the room and shouted, "I object! You learned men...you experts! Fooey on you. The explanation of the writings is quite simple. Everyone knows that Hebrews don't read from left to right, but from right to left.

"Now, look again ... what it really says is ... "HOLY MACKEREL, DIG THE ASS ON THAT WOMAN."

The Holiday Split

A Jewish father, in his 80s, living in Florida, calls his son, in New York, and says, " I hate to tell you, but we've got some troubles here in the house. Your mother and I can't stand each other anymore, and we are divorcing. That's it!!! I want to live out the rest of my years in peace. I am telling you now, so you and your sister shouldn't go into shock later when I move out."

He hangs up, and the son immediately calls his sister in and tells her the news. The sister says, "I'll handle this." She calls Florida and gets her father, on the phone. She pleads to her father, "Don't do ANYTHING until we get there! We will be there Friday night."

The father says, "All right, all right already."

He hangs up the phone, and hollers to his wife, "Okay, they're coming for Rosh Hashanah. Now, what are we going to tell them for Passover?"

In London, do as the British Do...

A man of the Jewish faith stopped at a posh gourmet food shoppe.on Regent Street in London. An impressive salesperson in morning coat with tails approached him and politely asked.
"Can I help you, Sir?"

"Yes," replied the customer, "I would like to buy a pound of lox."

"No, No," responded the dignified salesperson, "you mean smoked salmon."

"Okay, a pound of smoked salmon."

"Anything else?"

"Yes, a dozen blintzes."

"No. No. You mean crepes."

"Okay, a dozen crepes." "Anything else?"

"Yes. A pound of chopped liver."

"No. No. You mean pate."

"Okay," said the Jewish patron, "a pound of pate and," he added, "I'd like you to deliver this to my house on Saturday."

"Look," retorted the indignant salesperson, "we don't schlep on Shabbos!"

Talmudical Reasoning

For those of the Jewish faith, the Talmud is the commentary that explains the unexplainable, a guide to reason. As an example...

After months of negotiation with the authorities, a Talmudist from Odessa was granted permission to visit Moscow. He boarded the train and found an empty seat.

At the next stop a young man got on and sat next to him. The scholar looked at the young man and mused: This fellow doesn't look like a peasant, and if he isn't a peasant he probably comes from this district.

If he comes from this district, then he must be Jewish because this is, after all, a Jewish district. On the other hand, if he is a Jew, where could he be going? I'm the only Jew in our district who has permission to travel to Moscow. Ahh? But just outside Moscow there is a little village called Samvet, and Jews don't need special permission to go there.

But why would he be going to Samvet? He's probably going to visit one of the Jewish families there, but how many Jewish families are there in Samvet? Only two - the Bernsteins and the Steinbergs.

The Bernsteins are a terrible family, and a nice looking fellow like him must be visiting the Steinbergs. But why is he going? The Steinbergs have only daughters, so maybe he's their son-in-law. But if he is, then which daughter did he marry? They say that Sarah married a nice lawyer from Budapest, and Esther married a businessman from Zhitomer, so it must be Sarah's husband. Which means that his name is Alexander Cohen, if I'm not mistaken.

But if he comes from Budapest, with all the anti-Semitism they have there, he must have changed his name. What's the Hungarian equivalent of Cohen?

It's Kovacs. But if they allowed him to change his name, he must have some special status. What could it be? A doctorate from the University!

At this point the scholar turns to the young man and says, "How do you do, Dr. Kovacs?"

"Very well, thank you, sir," answered the startled passenger. "But how is it that you know my name?"

"Oh," replied the Talmudist, "it was obvious."

Jewish Truths Not Found in the Talmud

The optimist sees the bagel. The pessimist sees the hole.

If you can't say something nice, say it in Yiddish.

If it tastes good, it's probably not kosher.

No one looks good in a yarmulke.

Who else could have invented the 50 minute hour?

Why spoil a good meal with a big tip?

WASPs leave and never say good-bye. Jews say good-bye and never leave.

Twenty percent off is a bargain. Fifty percent off is a mitzvah (wonderful thing).

Wine needs to breathe, so don't rush through the kiddush.

Israel is the land of milk and honey; Florida is the land of milk of magnesia.

Never pay retail.

It's always a bad hair day if you're bald.

No one leaves a Jewish wedding hungry; but then again, no one leaves with a hangover.

The High Holidays have absolutely nothing to do with marijuana.

If your name was Lipschitz, you'd change it, too.

One mitzvah can change the world; two will just make you tired.

If you don't eat, it will kill me.

Anything worth saying is worth repeating a thousand times.

The most important word to know in any language is SALE.

Where there's smoke, there may be smoked salmon.

Never take a front-row seat at a Bris.

Prune Danish is definitely an acquired taste.

Next year in Jerusalem. The year after that, how about a nice cruise?

Never leave a restaurant empty-handed.

A bad matzoh ball makes a good paperweight.

A schmata is a dress that your husband's ex is wearing.

Without Jewish mothers, who would need therapy?

Before you read the menu, read the prices.

There comes a time in every man's life when he must stand up and tell his mother he's an adult. This usually happens at around age 45.

According to Jewish dietary law, pork and shellfish may be eaten only in Chinese restaurants

Tsouris is a Yiddish word that means your child is marrying someone who isn't Jewish.

If you're going to whisper at the movies, make sure it's loud enough for everyone to hear.

No meal is complete without leftovers.

What business is a yenta in? Yours.

If you have to ask the price, you can't afford it. But if you can afford it, make sure you tell everybody what you paid.

Prozac is like chicken soup: it doesn't cure anything, but it makes you feel better.

More than a Bris

A Jewish man was in an accident and his penis was chopped off. He was rushed to the hospital where the doctor examined him, and after careful examination said, "We can replace it with a small size penis for $5,000, a medium size one for $15,000, or an extra-large size penis for $30,000. I realize it's a lot of money, so take your time and talk it over with your wife."

When the doctor came back into the room he found the man staring sadly at the floor. "My wife says she'd rather have a new kitchen."

Groaners, a Jewish Tradition!

or Don't Blame Me, Blame My E-Mail

It seems a group of leading medical experts have published data that says that seder participants should NOT partake of both chopped liver and charoses. Their findings appear to indicate that this combination can lead to Charoses of the Liver.

At our seder, we had whole wheat and bran matzo, fortified with Metamucil. The brand name of this matzo is "Let My People Go."

What do you call steaks ordered by 10 Jews? .....Filet minyan

If a doctor carries a black bag and a plumber carries a tool box, what does a "mohel" carry? ....A Bris-kit!

What did the waiter ask the group of dining Jewish mothers? "Is ANYTHING all right?"

The Kosher Computer

The Rabbi came over yesterday and we had a Bris for my computer taking a little piece off the tail of the mouse. If you or a friend are considering a kosher computer, you should know that there were about 15 changes as follows:

1. I had to have two hard drives, one for fleyshedik business software and one for milchedik games.
2. Instead of getting a "General Protection Fault" error, my PC now gets "Ferklempt."
3. The Chanukah screen savers include "Flying Dreidels".
4 My PC also shuts down automatically at sundown on Friday evenings.
5. After my computer dies, I have to dispose of it within 24 hours.
6. My "Start" button has been replaced with a "Let's Go! I'm Not Getting Any Younger!" button.
7. When disconnecting external devices from the back of my PC, I am instructed to "Remove the cable from the PC's tuchus."
8. The multimedia player has been renamed to "Nu, so play my music already!"
9. Internet Explorer has a spinning "Star of David" in the upper right corner.
10. I hear "Hava Nagila" during startup.
11. Microsoft Office now includes "A little byte of this, and a little byte of that."
12. When my PC is working too hard, I occasionally hear a loud "Oy ,Gevalt!"
13. I saw a "monitor cleaning solution" from Manischewitz that advertises that it gets rid of the "schmutz und drek" on your monitor.
14. After 20 minutes of no activity, my PC goes "schloffen."
15. A computer virus can now be cured with some matzo ball chicken soup.
16. And the Y2K problem? It's been replaced by Year 5760-5761"issues.

Quotable from Notables

Most Texans think Hanukkah is some sort of duck call. -Richard Lewis

My father never lived to see his dream come true of an all-Yiddish-speaking Canada. -David Steinberg

I once wanted to become an atheist but I gave up....they have no holidays. -Henny Youngman

A Funny Thing Happened on the Way to the Health Fair

Look at Jewish history. Unrelieved lamenting would be intolerable. So, for every ten Jews beating their breasts, God designated one to be crazy and amuse the breast beaters. By the time I was five I knew I was that one. -Mel Brooks

The time is at hand when the wearing of a prayer shawl and skullcap will not bar a man from the White House, unless, of course, the man is Jewish. -Jules Farber

Even if you are Catholic, if you live in New York you're Jewish. If you live in Butte, Montana, you are going to be goyish even if you are Jewish. -Lenny Bruce

God, I know we are your chosen people, but couldn't you choose somebody else for a change? Tevye speech from "Fiddler on the Roof." -Shalom Aleichem

The remarkable thing about my mother is that for thirty years she served us nothing but leftovers. The original meal has never been found. -Calvin Trillin

Let me tell you the one thing I have against Moses. He took us forty years into the desert in order to bring us to the one place in the Middle East that has no oil! -Golda Meir

Even a secret agent can't lie to a Jewish mother. -Peter Malkin

Humility is no substitute for a good personality. -Fran Lebowitz

My idea of an agreeable person is a person who agrees with me. -Benjamin Disraeli

It's so simple to be wise. Just think of something stupid to say and then don't say it. -Sam Levenson

Don't be humble. You are not that great. -Golda Meir

God will pardon me. It's His business. -Heinrich Heine

I went on a diet, swore off drinking and heavy eating, and in fourteen days I had lost exactly two weeks. -Joe E. Lewis

Bankruptcy is a legal proceeding in which you put your money in your pants pocket and give your coat to your creditors. -Sam Goldwyn

A spoken contract isn't worth the paper it's written on. -Sam Goldwyn

Everybody likes a kidder but nobody loans him money. -Arthur Miller

I have enough money to last me the rest of my life unless I buy something. -Jackie Mason

I don't want to achieve immortality through my work. I want to achieve immortality through not dying. -Woody Allen

Marriage is a wonderful institution. But who wants to live in an institution? -Groucho Marx

A politician is a man who will double cross that bridge when he comes to it. Oscar Levant

Too bad that all the people who know how to run this country are busy driving taxis and cutting hair. -George Burns

Liberals feel unworthy of their possessions. Conservatives feel they deserve everything they've stolen. -Mort Sahl

A committee is a group that keeps minutes and loses hours. -Milton Berle

I don't want any yes-men around me. I want everybody to tell me the truth, even if it costs them their jobs. -Sam Goldwyn

Television is a medium because it is neither rare nor well done. -Ernie Kovacs

With the collapse of vaudeville, new talent has no place to stink. -George Burns

When I bore people at a party, they think it is their fault. -Henry Kissinger

Rules for the Jewish New Year

On Rosh Hashanah, the Jewish New Year, there is a ceremony called Tashlich. Observant people of the Jewish faith traditionally go to the ocean (or a stream or river), pray, and then throw bread crumbs onto the water, so the fish can symbolically eat their sins. Some people have been known to ask what kind of bread crumbs should they throw:
For ordinary sinsWhite Bread
For exotic sinsFrench Bread
For particularly dark sinsPumpernickel

For complex sinsMulti-Grain
For twisted sinsPretzels
For tasteless sinsRice Cakes
For sins of indecisionWaffles
For sins committed in hasteMatzo
For sins of chutzpahFresh Bread
For the sin of substance abuse/marijuanaStoned Wheat
For the sin of substance abuse/heavy drugsPoppy Seed
For the sin of committing auto theftCaraway
For the sin of committing arsonToast
For the sin of passiveness when action is warrantedMilk Toast
For the sin of being ill-tempered/sulkySourdough
For the sin of cheating customersShortbread
For the sin of risking one's life unnecessarilyHero (Sub) Roll
For the sin of excessive use of ironyRye Bread
For the sin of telling bad jokesCorn Bread
For the sin of being money hungryRaw Dough
For the sin of war-mongering or causing injury or damage to othersTortes
For the sin of promiscuityHot Buns
For the sin of promiscuity with gentilesHot Cross Buns
For the sin of dovenning (praying) off tuneFlat Bread
For the sin of being holier than thouBagels
For the sin of indecent photographyCheese Cake
For the sin of over-eatingStuffing
For the sin of gamblingFortune Cookies
For the sin of abrasivenessGrits
For sins of pridePuff Pastry
For the sin of cheating with Nutrasweet and OlestraBaked Goods
For the sin of impetuousnessQuick Bread
For negligent slip upsBanana Bread
For the sin of dropping in without warningPopovers
For the sin of perfectionismAngel Food Cake
For the sin of being up-tight and irritableHigh-Fiber Muffins

Move Over Oscar... Here Come the Izzys

The following movies have been nominated for an Izzy

THE SIX CENTS - 3 Jews each put in their 2 cents worth

GOY STORY 2 - Jewish man divorces a shiksa, marries another

ISN'T SHE GEVALDIK - Yeshiva boys read Jacqueline Susann

SUPERNOVA - Space scientists discover powerful strains of lox
SNOW FALLING ON SEDERS - Unexpected storm disrupts Passover

ANGELA'S KASHAS - Woman reveals secret recipe

GIRLS, INTERRUPTED - Women's section of shul shushed during dovening

STUART LADLE - Mouse makes chicken soup on Shabbos

THE SEDER HOUSE RULES - Zadie lays down the law on Pesach

THE TALMUDIC MR. RIPLEY - Believe it or not, he knows gemorah

Actual Personals That Appeared in Israeli Papers

Are you the girl I spoke with at the kiddush after shul last week? You excused yourself to get more horseradish for your gefilte fish, but you never returned. How can I contact you again? (I was the one with the maror stain on my tie).

Shochet, 54, owns successful butcher shop in Midwest. Doesn't believe women should be treated like a piece of meat.

Divorced Jewish man, seeks partner to attend shul with, light candles, celebrate holidays, build Sukkah together, attend brisses, bar mitzvahs. Religion is not important.

Sincere rabbinical student, 27. Enjoys Yom Kippur, Tisha B'av, Taanah Esther, Tzom Gedaliah, Asarah B'Teves, Shiva Asar B'Tammuz. Seeks companion for living life in the "fast" lane.

Yeshiva bochur, Torah scholar, long beard, payos. Seeks same in woman.

Worried about in-law meddling? I'm an orphan! Write.

Nice Jewish guy, 38. No skeletons. No baggage. No personality.

Female graduate student, studying kaballah, Zohar, exorcism of dybbuks, seeks mensch. No weirdos, please.

Staunch Jewish feminist, wears tzitzis, seeking male who will accept my independence, although you probably will not. Oh, just forget it

Jewish businessman, 49, manufactures Sabbath candles, Chanukah candles, Havdallah candles, Yahrzeit candles. Seeks non-smoker.

Israeli professor, 41, with 18 years of teaching in my behind. Looking for American-born woman who speaks English very good.

80-year-old bubbie, no assets, seeks handsome, virile Jewish male, under 35. Object matrimony. I can dream, can't I?

I am a sensitive Jewish prince to whom you can open your heart. Share your innermost thoughts and deepest secrets. Confide in me. I'll understand your insecurities. No fatties, please.

Jewish male, 34, very successful, smart, independent, self-made. Looking for girl whose father will hire me.

Single Jewish woman, 29, into disco, mountain climbing, skiing, track and field. Has slight limp.

Jewish Princess, 28, seeks successful businessman of any major Jewish denomination: hundreds, fifties, twenties.

Desperately seeking shmoozing! Retired senior citizen desires female companion 70+ for kvetching, kvelling, and krechtzing. Under 30 is also OK.

Attractive Jewish woman, 35, college graduate, seeks successful Jewish Prince Charming to get me out of my parents' house.

Shul gabbai, 36. I take out the Torah Saturday morning. Would like to take you out Saturday night. Please write.

Couch potato Latke, in search of the right applesauce. Let's try it for eight days. Who knows?

Who Wants To Be a Millionaire

For $500
Q. Who is Israel's favorite Internet provider?
A. Netan Yahoo.

For $1,000
Q. What is the name of a facial lotion made for Jewish women?
A. Oil of Oy Vey.

For $2,000
Q. What is the title of the new horror film for Jewish women?
A. Debbie Does Dishes.

For $4,000
Q. What is the technical term for a divorced Jewish Woman?
A. The "Plaintiff."

For $8,000
Q. How does a Jewish kid orally abuse his playmates?
A. "Your mother pays retail."

For $16,000
Q. In the Jewish doctrine, when does the fetus become human?
A. When it graduates from medical school.

For $32,000
Q. What does a Jewish woman do to keep her hands soft and her nails long and beautiful?
A. Nothing, she does nothing at all.

For $64,000
Q. Define "Genius."
A. A "C" student with a Jewish mother.

For $125,000
Q. What do you call a bloodthirsty Jew on a rampage?
A. Genghis Cohen.

For $250,000
Q. When does a Mohel retire?
A. When he just can't cut it anymore.

For $500,000
Q. If Tarzan and Jane were Jewish, what would Cheetah be?
A. A fur coat.

For $1,000,000
Q. What is the difference between a Jewish Grandmother and an Italian Grandmother?
A. 10 lbs

Come Back Sermon

A Rabbi was opening his mail one morning. Taking a single sheet of paper from an envelope he found written on it only one word: "SCHMUCK"

The next Friday night, from the pulpit, he announced, "I have known many people who have written letters and forgot to sign their names. But, this week, I received a letter from someone who signed his name and forgot to write a letter."

IRS Audit

A young hotshot gets a job with the IRS. His first assignment is to audit an old rabbi. He thinks he'll have a little fun with the old guy. The hotshot says, "Rabbi, what do you do with the drippings from the candles?"

The rabbi replies, "We send them to the candle factory, and every once in a while they send us a little candle."

The kid says, "And what do you do after the sermon with the paper you use?"

The rabbi says, "We send them to the paper factory for recycling. And every once in a while they send us a little package of paper."

The IRS guy asks, "And what do you do with the foreskins from your circumcisions?"

The rabbi answers, "We send them to the IRS, and every once in a while they send us a little schmuck like you."

Not to Worry

Morris and Esther, an elderly Jewish couple, are sitting together on an airplane flying to the Far East. Over the public address system, the Captain announces: "Ladies and Gentlemen, I am afraid I have some very bad news. Our engines have ceased functioning properly, and this plane will be going down. Luckily, I see an island below us that should be able to accommodate our landing. This island appears to be uncharted; I am unable to find it on our maps. So the odds are that we will never be rescued and will have to live on the island for a very long time, if not for the rest of our lives."

A few minutes later the plane lands safely, whereupon Morris turns to his wife and asks, "Esther, did we pay our pledge to the Yeshiva yet?"

"No, Morris!", she responded.

Morris smiles, then asks, "Esther, did we pay our United Jewish Appeal pledge?"

"Oh, no, I forgot to send the check!!"

Now Morris laughs.

Esther asks Morris, "So what are you smiling and laughing about?"

Morris responds, "They'll find us!!"

Bargaining with the Bubbie

A Jewish lady's grandson is playing in the water, she is standing on the beach not wanting to get her feet wet, when all of a sudden, a huge wave appears from nowhere and crashes directly over the spot where the boy is wading. The water recedes and the boy is no longer there. He simply vanished.

She holds her hands to the sky, screams and cries, "Lord, how could you? Have I not been a wonderful Grandmother? Have I not been a wonderful mother? Have I not given to Bnai Brith? Have I not given to Hadassah? Have I not lit candles every Friday night at dusk? Have I not tried my very best to live a life that you would be proud of?"

A loud voice booms from the sky, "Okay, okay!" A few minutes later another huge wave appears out of nowhere and crashes on the beach. As the water recedes, the boy is standing there, smiling, splashing around as if nothing had ever happened.

The loud voice booms again "I have returned your grandson. Are you satisfied?"

She responds, "He had a hat."

The Jewish Samurai

Back in the time of the Samurai there was a powerful emperor who needed a new chief Samurai, so he sent out a declaration throughout the country that he was searching for one.

A year passed, and only 3 people showed up: a Japanese Samurai, a Chinese Samurai, and a Jewish Samurai.

The emperor asked the Japanese Samurai to come in and demonstrate why he should be the chief Samurai. The Japanese Samurai opened a match box, and out popped a bumblebee. Whoosh! went his sword, and the bumblebee dropped dead on the ground in 2 pieces.

The emperor exclaimed, "That is impressive!"

The emperor then asked the Chinese Samurai to come in and demonstrate. The Chinese Samurai also opened a match box, and out buzzed a fly. Whoosh, Whoosh! went his sword, and the fly dropped dead on the ground in 4 small pieces.

The emperor exclaimed: "That is really VERY impressive!"

The emperor then had the Jewish Samurai demonstrate why he should be the head Samurai. The Jewish Samurai also opened a match box, and out flew a gnat. His flashing sword went Whooooosh!Whooooosh! But the gnat was still alive and flying around. The emperor, obviously disappointed, asked, "After all of that, why is the gnat not dead?"

The Jewish Samurai smiled. "Well," he replied, "circumcision is not meant to kill."

Tick-Tock Cut

An American tourist was visiting in the Netherlands. During his stay in Amsterdam his watch stopped running. He asked one of the locals where he could get his watch fixed. The tourist was guided to the Jewish section of town. He was then directed toward a shop that had clocks displayed in the window. The American tourist entered the shop. Inside, behind a desk, sat an elderly Jewish man with a full beard.

TOURIST: Hello.

JEWISH MAN: Hello.

TOURIST: I came here to have my watch fixed.

JEWISH MAN: Sorry, I don't fix watches. I am a Mohel.

TOURIST: What's a Mohel?

JEWISH MAN: A Mohel is a Jewish Man who performs ritual circumcisions.

TOURIST: Ritual circumcisions! But why do you have all those clocks in the window?

JEWISH MAN: So what would you want me to have in my window?

A Moishe by Any Other Name

Walking through San Francisco's Chinatown, a tourist from the Midwest was fascinated with all
the Chinese restaurants, shops, signs and banners. He turned a corner and saw a building with the sign "Moishe Plotnik's Chinese Laundry."

"Moishe Plotnik?" he wondered. "How does that fit in Chinatown?" Curious, he walked into the shop and saw a fairly standard looking Chinese laundry.

He could see that the proprietor was clearly aware of the uniqueness of the name as there were baseball hats, T-Shirts and coffee mugs emblazoned with the logo "Moishe Plotnik's Chinese Laundry."

There was also a fair selection of Chinatown souvenirs, indicating that the name alone had brought many tourists into the shop. The tourist selected a coffee cup as a conversation piece to take back to his office.

Behind the counter was a smiling old Chinese gentleman who thanked him for his purchase in English, thickly accented with Chinese. The tourist asked, "Can you tell me how this place got a name like "Moishe Plotnik's Chinese Laundry?"

The old man answered, "Ahh... Everybody ask, 'That is name of owner?'." Looking around, the tourist asked, "Is he here now?"

"He is right here," replied the old man. "He is me."

"Really? How did you ever get a name like Moishe Plotnik?"

"Is simple," said the old man. "Many, many year ago when come to this country, I was stand in line at Documentation Center. Man in front is Jewish gentleman from Poland. Lady look at him and say, 'What your name?' " He say, 'Moishe Plotnik.'"

"Then she look at me and say, 'What your name?'

"I say, 'Sam Ting.'"

Carry-Out

A Hebrew teacher stood in front of his classroom and said, "The Jewish people have observed their 5,759th year as a people. Consider that the Chinese, for example, have only observed their
4,692nd year as a people. What does that mean to you?"

After a moment of silence, one student raised his hand. "Yes, David," the teacher said, "What does that mean?"

"It means that the Jews had to do without Chinese food for 1,067 years."

The Wall

A journalist assigned to the Jerusalem bureau takes an apartment overlooking the Wailing Wall. Every day when she looks out, she sees an old Jewish man praying vigorously.

So the journalist goes down to the wall, and introduces herself to the old man. She asks: "You come every day to the wall. How long have you done that and what are you praying for?"

The old man replies, "I have come here to pray every day for 25 years. In the morning I pray for world peace and then for the brotherhood of man. I go home have a cup of tea, and I come back and pray for the eradication of illness and disease from the earth."

The journalist is amazed. "How does it make you feel to come here every day for 25 years and pray for these things?" she asks.

The old man replies, calmly...."Like I'm talking to a wall."

So, Nu, As Time Goes By

You must remember this,
A bris is still a bris,
A chai is just a chai.

Pastrami still belongs on rye,
As time goes by.

With holidays in view,
A Jew is still a Jew,
On that you can rely.

No matter if we eat tofu
As time goes by.

Old shtetl customs, never out of date.
All those potatoes someone has to grate.
One flame in the window,
keep counting 'til there's eight
To light the winter sky.

In the Bronx or in the Mission,
It's still the same tradition,
That no one can deny.

We roam, but we recall our birthright,
As time goes by.

Dreidels and chocolate, never out of date.
Ancient Semitic glories to relate.
Blue-and-white giftwrap, ain't this country great,
And festive chazerai!

It's still the same old Torah,
It's still the same menorah,
We've latkes still to fry.

December's when I feel most Jewish,
As time goes by

The Social Thing to Do... or Not

A modern Orthodox Jewish couple, preparing for a religious wedding, meets with their rabbi for Counseling. The rabbi asks if they have any last questions before they leave.

The man asks, "Rabbi, we realize it's tradition for men to dance with men, and women to dance with women at the reception. But, we'd like your permission to dance together."

"Absolutely not!", says the rabbi. "It's immodest. Men and women always dance separately."

Groom to be: "Even after the ceremony I can't even dance with my own wife?"

"No,", answered the rabbi. "it's forbidden!"

"Well, what about sex?"asks the man. "Can we finally have sex?"

"Of course!" replies the rabbi. "Sex is a mitzvah (a blessing) within marriage, to have children!"

"What about different positions?", asks the man.

"No problem," says the rabbi. "It's a mitzvah!"

"Woman on top?", the man asks.

"Sure." says the rabbi. "Go for it! It's a mitzvah!"

"On the kitchen table?"

"Yes, yes! A mitzvah!"

"Can we do it on rubber sheets with a bottle of hot oil, a couple of vibrators, a leather harness, a bucket of honey and a porno video?"

"You may indeed. It's all a mitzvah!"

"Can we do it standing up?"

"NO!", cries the rabbi.

"Why not?"

"It could lead to dancing."

Grandma's Cruise

The children and grandchildren of an elderly Jewish woman decided to send Bubbe (grandmother) on a cruise. Bubbe boarded the ship and showed her ticket to the purser. He looked at it and said, "Oh, I see you have U.D."

She replied, "U.D.? Voos is a U.D.?

He said, "U.D. is Upper Deck."

She then went to the upper deck and showed her ticket a ship's officer he said, "I see, that you have O.C."

Bubbe replied, "O.C.? Voos is O.C.?"
The officer said, "O.C. is Outside Cabin."

Bubbe, needless to say, was delighted. She then showed her ticket to the Cabin Stewart and he said, "Oh, I see that you have B.I.B."

"B.I.B..? Voos is B.I.B.?" asked Bubbe.

The Cabin Stewart answered, "B.I.B. is a request for Breakfast In Bed."

Well, the next morning, bright and early, the Stewart came right into her room with a tray of food for her breakfast in bed and she said, "F.U.C.K."

Shocked, the Stewart said, "F.U.C.K? What do you mean F.U.C.K.?", to which she replied, "Yes, F.U.C.K... First U Could Knock!"

The Real Meaning of Yenta

Four Jewish ladies were sitting around playing Mahjongg. The first lady says, "You know girls, I have known you all for such a long time, and there is something I must get off my chest. I am a Kleptomaniac. But don't worry, I have never stolen from any of you and never will. We have been friends for too long."

One of the other ladies says, "Well since were having true confessions I am a Nymphomaniac. But don't worry, I have not hit on any of your husbands, and never will. They don't interest me. We have been friends for too long."

"Well," says the third lady, "I too must confess. The reason I never married is that I am a Lesbian, but don't worry. I will never hit on any of you.You all are not my type. We have been friends for too long, and I don't want to ruin our friendship."

The fourth lady stands up and says: "I have a confession to make also. I am a Yenta, so please excuse me, I have a lot of calls to make."

To Make Lemonade

The local bar owner was so sure that his bartender was the strongest man around that the owner offered a standing $1,000 bet that the bartender would squeeze a lemon until all the juice ran into a glass, and hand the lemon to a patron. If anyone who could squeeze one more drop of juice out of the lemon would win the money. Many people had tried over time, weight lifters, longshoremen, wrestlers, and the like, but nobody could do it.

One day this scrawny little man wearing thick glasses and a polyester suit came in and announced in a tiny, squeaky voice, "I'd like to try the bet."

After the laughter had died down, the bartender said, "OK," grabbed a lemon and squeezed away. He then handed the wrinkled remains of the rind to the little man.

The crowd's laughter turned to silence as the man clenched his fist around the lemon and six drops fell into the glass. As the crowd cheered, the bartender paid the $1,000, and asked the little man, "What do you do for a living? Are you a lumberjack, a weight lifter, or what?"

The man replied, "I'm a fund raiser for the United Jewish Appeal."

Wisdom from Sam Levinson

"It's a free world and you don't have to like Jews, but if you DON'T, I suggest that you boycott certain Jewish products, like .....
The Wasserman Test for syphilis, Digitalis, discovered by Doctor Nuslin, Insulin, discovered by Doctor Minofsky, Chloral Hydrate, discovered by Doctor Lifreich, The Schick Test for Diphtheria, Vitamins, discovered by

Doctor Funk, Streptomycin, discovered by Doctor Woronan, The Polio
Pill by Doctor Sabin, and the Polio Vaccine by Doctor Jonas Salk.

Go on, boycott! Humanitarian consistency requires that my people offer
all these gifts to all people of the world.

Fanatic consistency requires that all bigots accept Syphilis, Diabetes,
Convulsions, Malnutrition,
Infantile Paralysis and Tuberculosis as a matter of principal.

You want to be mad at us? Be mad at us! But I'm telling you, you ain't
going to feel so good

Section 14: News at 11

How Strange is Truth?

Down Under

From the Sydney Morning Herald Australia comes this story of a central west couple who drove their car to K-Mart only to have their car break down in the parking lot. The man told his wife to carry on with the shopping while he fixed the car. The wife returned later to see a small group of people near the car. On closer inspection she saw a pair of male legs protruding from under the chassis.

Although the man was in shorts, his lack of underpants turned private parts into glaringly public ones. Unable to stand the embarrassment she dutifully stepped forward and tucked everything back into place. On regaining her feet she looked across the hood and found herself staring at her husband who was standing idly by. The mechanic, however, had to have three stitches in his head.

All That Glitters

This is for all those women out there who so look forward to that wonderful time, once a year, when they get to be "intimate" with their OB/GYN doctor! In Sydney, Australia one of the radio stations pays money ($1000 up to $5000) for people to tell their most embarrassing stories. This one netted the winner $5000...

"I was due later in the week for an appointment with the gynecologist. Early one morning I received a call from the doctor's office to tell me that I had been rescheduled for early that morning -- 9:30 a.m. I had only just packed everyone off to work and school, and it was already around 8:45 a.m.

"The trip to his office took about 35 minutes, so I didn't have any time to spare. As most women do, I like to take a little extra effort over hygiene when making such visits, but this time I wasn't going to be able to make the full effort. So I rushed upstairs, threw off my dressing gown, wet the washcloth that was sitting next to the sink, and gave myself a quick wash in "that area" to make sure I was at least presentable.

"I threw the washcloth in the clothes basket, donned some clothes, hopped in the car and raced to my appointment. I was in the waiting room only a few minutes when I was called in. Knowing the procedure, as I'm sure you do, I hopped up on the table, looked over at the other side of the room and pretended I was in Paris or some other place a million miles away.

"I was a little surprised when the doctor said, "My, we have made an extra effort this morning, haven't we?" But I didn't respond.

"When the appointment was over, I heaved a sigh of relief and went home. The rest of the day was normal - some shopping, cleaning, cooking, etc. After school, while my six-year-old daughter was playing, she called out from the bathroom, "Mum, where's my washcloth?"

I told her to get another one from the cupboard. "No!" she replied. "I need the one that was here
by the sink. It had all my glitter and sparkles in it."

Southern Nativity Scene

Passing through a small Southern town one evening last December, I was impressed to see a Nativity Scene that showed great skill and talent had gone into creating it. It was so beautiful that I got out of my car for a closer look. One small feature did bother me, though: The three Wise Men seemed to be wearing firemen helmets. Totally unable to come up with a reason or explanation, I left, pondering.

At a "QuikStop" on the edge of town, I asked the lady behind the counter about the helmets. She exploded into a rage, yelling at me, "Y'all Yankees never do read the Bible!" I assured her that I did, but simply couldn't recall anything about firemen in the Bible. She jerked her Bible
from behind the counter and ruffled through some pages, and finally jabbed her finger at a passage. Sticking the Bible in my face, she announced triumphantly, "See, it says right here...The three wise men came from afar."

Have a Cigar!

A Charlotte, North Carolina man having purchased a box of very rare and expensive cigars then insured them against fire among other things. Within a month having smoked his entire stockpile of these great cigars and without yet having made even his first premium payment on the policy, the man filed a claim against the insurance company. In his claim, the man stated the cigars were lost "in a series of small fires."

The insurance company refused to pay, citing the obvious reason - the man had consumed the cigars in the normal fashion. The man sued....and won!

In delivering the ruling the judge agreed with the insurance company that the claim was frivolous. The Judge stated nevertheless, that the man held a policy from the company in which it had warranted that the cigars were insurable and also guaranteed that it would insure them against fire, without defining what is considered to be "unacceptable fire," and was obligated to pay the claim.

Rather than endure a lengthy and costly appeal process, the insurance company accepted the ruling and paid $15,000.00 to the man for his loss of the rare cigars lost in the "fires."

After the man cashed the check, the insurance company had him arrested on 24 counts of ARSON!!!! With his own insurance claim and testimony from the previous case being used against him, the man was convicted of intentionally burning his insured property and sentenced him to 24 months in jail and a $24,000.00 fine.

This is a true story and was the 1st place winner in a recent Criminal Lawyers Darwin Award Contest.

As Reported in a Newspaper...

Police arrested Patrick Lawrence, a 22-year-old white male, resident of Dacula, GA, in a pumpkin patch at 11:38 p.m. Friday. Lawrence will be charged with lewd and lascivious behavior, public indecency, and public intoxication at the Gwinnett County courthouse on Monday. The suspect allegedly stated that as he was passing a pumpkin patch, he decided to stop. "You know, a pumpkin is soft and squishy inside, and there was no one around here for miles. At least I thought there wasn't," he stated in a phone interview from the Lawrenceville jail.

Lawrence went on to state that he pulled over to the side of the road picked out a pumpkin that he felt was appropriate to his purposes, cut a hole in it, and proceeded to satisfy his alleged "need." "I guess I was just really into it, you know?" he commented with evident embarrassment.

In the process, Lawrence apparently failed to notice the Gwinnett County police car approaching and was unaware of his audience until officer Brenda Taylor approached him. "It was an unusual situation, that's for sure," said officer Taylor. "I walked up to (Lawrence) and he's just working away at this pumpkin."

Taylor went on to describe what happened when she approached

Lawrence. "I just went up and said, "Excuse me sir, but do you realize that you are screwing a pumpkin?" He got real surprised, as you'd expect, and then looked me straight in the face and said, "A pumpkin? Damn...is it midnight already?"

Edited by Fred Neil

Section: Fifteen
It's on the List

Lists, Lists, and More Lists

Here are actual quotes taken from Federal Employee Performance Evaluations.

1. "Since my last report, this employee has reached rock bottom and has started to dig."

2. "I would not allow this employee to breed."

3. "This employee is really not so much of a has-been, but more of a definite won't be."

4. "Works well when under constant supervision and cornered like a rat in a trap."

5. "When she opens her mouth, it seems that it is only to change feet."

6. "He would be out of his depth in a parking lot puddle."

7. "This young lady has delusions of adequacy."

8. "He sets low personal standards and then consistently fails to achieve them."

9. "This employee is depriving a village somewhere of an idiot."

10. "This employee should go far, and the sooner he starts the better."

11. "Got a full 6 pack, but lacks the plastic thing to hold it all together."

12. "A gross ignoramus. . .144 times worse than an ordinary ignoramus."

13. "He doesn't have ulcers, but he's a carrier."

14. "I would like to go hunting with him sometime."

15. "He's been working with glue too much."

16. "He would argue with a signpost."

17. "He brings a lot of joy whenever he leaves the room."

18. "When his IQ reaches 50 he should sell."

19. "If you see two people talking and one looks bored, he's the other one."

20. "A photographic memory but with the lens cover glued on."

21. "A prime candidate for natural de-selection."

22. "Donated his brain to science before he was done using it."

23. "Gates are down, the lights are flashing, but the train isn't coming."

24. "He's got two brains, one is lost and the other is out looking for it."

25. "If he were any more stupid, he'd have to be watered twice a week

26. "If you give him a penny for his thoughts, you'd get change.

27. "If you stand close enough to him, you can hear the ocean."

28. "It's hard to believe he beat out 1,000,000 other sperm."

29. "One neuron short of a synapse."

30. "Some drink from the fountain of knowledge; he only gargled."

31. "Takes him 2 hours to watch 60 minutes."

32. "The wheel is turning, but the hamster is dead."

Ten Signs Your Dot.Com Firm is on the Skids

1. The company CEO has moved from the corner office to the ledge outside the corner office.

2. The manager informs you that the drinks in the company fridge haven't been free and hands you a $4,800 Snapple bill.

3. The company president asks if anyone has a problem giving out a little astrological advice over the phone while they work.

4. The head of Research and Development is spending more and more

time in the park across street with a metal detector he refers to as his "search engine."

5. There's now 10-year-old Indonesian boys on either side of you assembling Nike running shoes.

6. Management is now using copies of the company prospectus exclusively for toilet paper.

7. Next time you see the company's founder, he is wearing a paper hat and telling you which one is the Diet Coke.

8. The human resources manager informs you that (though it wasn't spelled out in black and white) giving conventioneers body massages was indeed implied in your job description, and that it could also involve a little "converging," if you know what he means.

9. You arrive at work to find that all the computers have been replaced with Etch-a-Sketches.

10. Your boss concedes that he might be out of his teens before he's able to retire.

List of Signs

Veterinarian's Office sign: All unattended children will be given a free kitten.

Plumber's Shop: We repair what your husband fixed.

Pizza Shop slogan: 7 days without pizza makes one weak.

At a tire shop in Milwaukee: Invite us to your next blowout.

Sign at the Psychic's Hotline: Don't call us, we'll call you.

At a Towing Company: We don't charge an arm and a leg. We want tows.

Billboard on the side of the road: Keep your eyes on the road and stop reading these signs.

On an Electrician's Business: Let us remove your shorts.

In a Veterinarian's Office: Be back in 5 minutes, Sit! Stay!

In a Nonsmoking Area: If we see smoking we will assume you are on fire and take appropriate action.

On Maternity Room Door: Push, Push, Push.

At an Optometrist's Office: If you don't see what you're looking for you've come to the right place.

On a Taxidermist's window: We really know our stuff.

In a Podiatrist's Office: Time wounds all heels.

On a fence: Salesmen Welcome: Dog food is expensive.

Outside a Muffler Shop: No appointment necessary, we'll hear you coming.

Inside a Bowling Alley: Please be quiet, we need to hear a pin drop.

Lot outside Veterinarian's Office: Parking for Customers Only, all others will be Neutered.

Next - Trivia!

1. The first couple to be shown in bed together on prime time TV were Fred and Wilma Flintstone.

2. Coca-Cola was originally green.

3. Every day more money is printed for Monopoly than the US Treasury.

4. Men can read smaller print than women can; women can hear better.

5. The state with the highest percentage of people who walk to work: Alaska

6. The percentage of Africa that is wilderness: 28%

7. The percentage of North America that is wilderness: 38%

8. The cost of raising a medium-size dog to the age of eleven: $6,400

9. The average number of people airborne over the U.S. any given hour:

61,000

10. Intelligent people have more zinc and copper in their hair.

11. The world's youngest parents were 8 and 9 and lived in China in 1910.

12. The youngest Pope was 11 years old.

13. The first novel ever written on a typewriter: Tom Sawyer.

14. Those San Francisco Cable cars are the only mobile National Monuments.

15. Each king in a deck of playing cards represents a great king from history:

> Spades - King David
> Hearts - Charlemagne
> Clubs - Alexander the Great
> Diamonds - Julius Caesar

16. $111,111,111 \times 111,111,111 = 12,345,678,987,654,321$

17. If a statue in the park of a person on a horse has both front legs in the air, the person died in battle. If the horse has one front leg in the air, the person died as a result of wounds received in battle. If the horse has all four legs on the ground, the person died of natural causes.

18. Only two people signed the Declaration of Independence on July 4th, John Hancock and Charles Thomson. Most of the rest signed on August 2, but the last signature wasn't added until 5 years later.

20. "I am." is the shortest complete sentence in the English language.

21. Hershey's Kisses are called that because the machine that make them looks as if it's kissing the conveyor belt.

22. No NFL team which plays its home games in a domed stadium has ever won a Super bowl. until 1999.

23. The only two days of the year in which there are no major professional sports games (MLB, NBA, NHL, or NFL) are the day before and the day after the Major League all-stars Game. (That may change.)

24. The nursery rhyme "Ring around the Rosey" is a rhyme about the plague. Infected people with the plague would get red circular sores ("Ring around the rosy..."), these sores would smell very bad, so common

folks would put flowers on their bodies somewhere (inconspicuously) so that they would cover the smell of the sores ("...a pocket full of posies..."). People who died from the plague would be burned so as to reduce the possible spread of the disease ("...ashes, ashes, we all fall down!").

Q. What occurs more often in December than any other month?
A. Conception.

Q. What separates "60 Minutes," on CBS from every other TV show?
A. No theme song.

Q. Half of all Americans live within 50 miles of what?
A. Their birthplace.

Q. Most boat owners name their boats. What is the most popular boat name requested?
A. Obsession

Q. If you were to spell out numbers, how far would you have to go until you would find the letter "A"?
A. One thousand

Q. What do bulletproof vests, fire escapes, windshield wipers, and laser printers all have in common?
A. All invented by women.

Q. What is the only food that doesn't spoil?
A. Honey
Q. There are more collect calls on this day than any other day of the year?
A. Father's Day

Q. What trivia fact about the late Mel Blanc (voice of Bugs Bunny) is the most ironic?
A. He was allergic to carrots.

Q. What is an activity performed by 40% of all people at a party?
A. Snoop in your medicine cabinet.

Source of this Trivia section: Editor's E-mail

Did you know ....

It is impossible to lick your elbow.

A crocodile can't stick its tongue out.

A shrimp's heart is in their head.

In a study of 200,000 ostriches over a period of 80 years, no one reported a single case where an ostrich buried its head in the sand (or attempted to do so)

It is physically impossible for pigs to look up into the sky.

A pregnant goldfish is called a twit

Between 1937 and 1945 Heinz produced a version of Alphabet Spaghetti especially for the German market that consisted solely of little pasta swastikas.

On average, a human being will have sex more than 3,000 times and spend two weeks kissing in their lifetime.

More than 50% of the people in the world have never made or received a telephone call.

Rats and horses can't vomit.

The "sixth sick sheik's sixth sheep's sick" is said to be the toughest tongue twister in the English language.

If you sneeze too hard, you can fracture a rib. If you try to suppress a sneeze, you can rupture a blood vessel in your head or neck and die. If you keep your eyes open by force, they can pop out.

Rats multiply so quickly that in 18 months, two rats could have over million descendants.

Wearing headphones for just an hour will increase the bacteria in your ear by 700 times.

If the government has no knowledge of aliens, then why does Title 14, Section 1211 of the Code of Federal Regulations, implemented on July 16, 1969, make it illegal for U.S. citizens to have any contact with extraterrestrials or their vehicles?

In every episode of Seinfeld there is a Superman somewhere.

The cigarette lighter was invented before the match.

Thirty-five percent of the people who use personal ads for dating are already married.

A duck's quack doesn't echo, and no one knows why.

23% of all photocopier faults worldwide are caused by people sitting on them and photocopying their buttocks.

In the course of an average lifetime you will, while sleeping, eat 70 assorted insects and 10 spiders.

Most lipstick contains fish scales.

Cat's urine glows under a black-light.

Like fingerprints, everyone's tongue print is different

Over 75% of people who read this will try to lick their elbow

Source of this Trivia section is also the Editor's E-mail

In Plain English

This was passed on by a linguist, original author unknown. It really does boggle the mind !!

Reasons why the English language is so hard to learn:

1) The bandage was wound around the wound.

2) The farm was used to produce produce.

3) The dump was so full that it had to refuse more refuse.

4) We must polish the Polish furniture.

5) He could lead if he would get the lead out.

6) The soldier decided to desert his dessert in the desert.

7) Since there is no time like the present, he thought it was time to present the present.

8) A bass was painted on the head of the bass drum.

9) When shot at, the dove dove into the bushes.

10) I did not object to the object.

11) The insurance was invalid for the invalid.

12) There was a row among the oarsmen about how to row.

13) They were too close to the door to close it.

14) The buck does funny things when the does are present.

15) A seamstress and a sewer fell down into a sewer line.

16) To help with planting, the farmer taught his sow to sow.

17) The wind was too strong to wind the sail.

18) After a number of injections my jaw got number.

19) Upon seeing the tear in the painting I shed a tear.

20) I had to subject the subject to a series of tests.

21) How can I intimate this to my most intimate friend?

Let's face it - English is a crazy language

There is no egg in eggplant nor ham in hamburger; neither apple nor pine in pineapple.

English muffins weren't invented in England or French fries in France. Sweetmeats are candies while sweetbreads, which aren't sweet, are meat.

We take English for granted. But if we explore its paradoxes, we find that quicksand can work slowly, boxing rings are square and a guinea pig is neither from Guinea nor is it a pig.

And why is it that writers write but fingers don't fing, grocers don't groce and hammers don't ham? If the plural of tooth is teeth, why isn't the plural of booth beeth?

One goose, 2 geese. So one moose, 2 meese?

One index, 2 indices? Doesn't it seem crazy that you can make amends but not one amend.

If you have a bunch of odds and ends and get rid of all but one of them, what do you call it? If teachers taught, why didn't preachers praught?

If a vegetarian eats vegetables, what does a humanitarian eat?

Sometimes I think all the English speakers should be committed to an asylum for the verbally insane. In what language do people recite at a play and play at a recital?

Ship by truck and send cargo by ship?

Have noses that run and feet that smell?

How can a slim chance and a fat chance be the same, while a wise man and a wise guy are opposites?

You have to marvel at the unique lunacy of a language in which your house can burn up as it burns down, in which you fill in a form by filling it out and in which, an alarm goes off by going on.

English was invented by people, not computers, and it reflects the creativity of the human race, which, of course, is not a race at all.

That is why, when the stars are out, they are visible, but when the lights are out, they are invisible.

PS. - Why doesn't "Buick" rhyme with "quick?"

Answers for Questions You Never Asked

Q: What's the best form of birth control after 50?
    A: Nudity.
Q. What's the difference between a girlfriend and a wife?
    A: 45 lb.
Q: What's the difference between a boyfriend and a husband?
    A: 45 minutes.

Q: How many women does it take to change a light bulb?

A: None, they just sit there in the dark and bitch.

Q: Why is it so hard for women to find men that are sensitive, caring, and good looking?

A: Because those men already have boyfriends.

Q: What's the difference between a new husband and a new dog?

A: After a year, the dog is still excited to see you.

Q: What makes men chase women they have no intention of marrying?

A: The same urge that makes dogs chase cars they have no intention of driving.

Q: What do you call a smart blonde?

A: A golden retriever.

Q: A brunette, a blonde, and a redhead are all in third grade. Who has the biggest boobs?

A: The blonde, because she's 18.

Q: Why don't bunnies make noise when they have sex?

A: Because they have cotton balls.

Q: What's the difference between a porcupine and a BMW?

A: A porcupine has the pricks on the outside.

Q: What did the blonde say when she found out she was pregnant?

A: "Are you sure it's mine?"

Q: What's the difference between Beer Nuts and Deer Nuts?

A: Beer Nuts are $1 and Deer Nuts are always under a buck.

Q: Why does Mike Tyson cry during sex?

A: Mace will do that to you.

Q: Why did OJ Simpson want to move to Kentucky?

A: Everyone has the same DNA.

Q: What would you call it when an Italian has one arm shorter than the other?

A: A speech impediment.

Q: Why do men find it difficult to make eye contact?

A: Breasts don't have eyes.

Q: What's the difference between a Southern zoo and a Northern zoo?

A: A Southern zoo has a description of the animal on the front of the cage - along with a recipe.

Q: What's the Cuban National Anthem?

A: Row, row, row your boat.

Q: What's the difference between a Northern fairy tale and a Southern fairy tale?

A: A Northern fairy tale begins "Once upon a time." A Southern fairy tale begins 'Y'all ain't gonna believe this shit."

Things My Mother Taught Me

TO APPRECIATE A JOB WELL DONE - "If you're going to kill each other, do it outside - I just finished cleaning!"

RELIGION - "You better pray that will come out of the carpet."

ABOUT TIME TRAVEL - "If you don't straighten up, I'm going to knock you into the middle of next week!"

LOGIC - "Because I said so, that's why."

FORESIGHT - "Make sure you wear clean underwear in case you're in an accident."

IRONY - "Keep laughing and I'll *give* you something to cry about."
ABOUT THE SCIENCE OF OSMOSIS - "Shut your mouth and eat your supper!"

ABOUT CONTORTIONISM - "Will you *look* at the dirt on the back of your neck!"

ABOUT STAMINA - "You'll sit there 'til all that spinach is finished."

ABOUT WEATHER - "It looks as if a tornado swept through your room."

HOW TO SOLVE PHYSICS PROBLEMS - "If I yelled because I saw a meteor coming toward you; would you listen then?"

ABOUT HYPOCRISY - "If I've told you once, I've told you a million times - Don't exaggerate!!!"

THE CIRCLE OF LIFE - "I brought you into this world, and I can take you out."

ABOUT BEHAVIOR MODIFICATION - "Stop acting like your father!"

ABOUT ENVY - "There are millions of less fortunate children in this world who don't have wonderful parents like you do!"

New Proverbs

If you're too open minded, your brains will fall out.

Age is a very high price to pay for maturity.

Before you criticize someone, walk a mile in his shoes. That way, if he gets angry, he'll be a mile away - and barefoot.

Going to church doesn't make you a Christian any more than going to a garage makes you a mechanic.

Artificial intelligence is no match for natural stupidity.

A clear conscience is usually the sign of a bad memory.

A closed mouth gathers no feet.

If you must choose between two evils, pick the one you've never tried before.

My idea of housework is to sweep the room with a glance.

Not one shred of evidence supports the notion that life is serious.

It is easier to get forgiveness than permission.

For every action, there is an equal and opposite government program.

If you look like your passport picture, you probably need the trip.

Always yield to temptation, because it may not pass your way again.

Bills travel through the mail at twice the speed of checks.

A conscience is what hurts when all your other parts feel so good.

Eat well, stay fit, die anyway.

Men are from earth. Women are from earth. Deal with it.

No husband has ever been shot while doing the dishes.

Rim Shots

At the cocktail party, one woman said to another, "Aren't you wearing your wedding ring on the wrong finger?" The other replied, "Yes, I am, I married the wrong man."

After a quarrel, a wife said to her husband, "You know, I was a fool when I married you." The husband replied, "Yes, dear, but I was in love and didn't notice."

A man inserted an Ad in the classifieds: "Wife wanted." Within two days he received a hundred letters. They all said the same thing: "You can have mine."

When a man steals your wife, there is no better revenge than to let him keep her.

Marriage is the triumph of imagination over intelligence. Second marriage is the triumph of hope over experience.

I married Miss Right. I just didn't know her first name was Always.

Losing a wife can be hard. In my case, it was almost impossible.

I haven't spoken to my wife in 18 months - I don't like to interrupt her.

Just think, if it weren't for marriage, men would go through life thinking they had no faults at all.

"You know what I did before I married? Anything I wanted to." Henny Youngman

"The best way to get most husbands to do something is to suggest that perhaps they're too old to do it." - Ann Bancroft

"Any husband who says, 'My wife and I are completely equal partners,' is talking about either a law firm or a hand of bridge." - Bill Cosby

"Keep your eyes wide open before marriage, half shut afterwards." - Benjamin Franklin

"My wife dresses to kill. She cooks the same way." Henny Youngman

"My wife and I were happy for twenty years. Then we met." - Rodney Dangerfield

"A good wife always forgives her husband when she's wrong." - Milton Berle

My girlfriend told me I should be more affectionate. So I got two girlfriends.

A husband said to his wife, "No, I don't hate your relatives. In fact, I like your mother-in-law better than I like mine."

How do most men define marriage? A very expensive way to get your laundry done free.

A man said his credit card was stolen but he decided not to report it because the thief was spending less than his wife did.

The most effective way to remember your wife's birthday is to forget it once.

First guy (proudly): "My wife's an angel!" Second guy: "You're lucky, mine's still alive."

Women will never be equal to men until they can walk down the street with a bald head and a beer gut, and still think they are beautiful!!!

"I was married by a judge. I should have asked for a jury." - George Burns

"What's the difference between a boyfriend and a husband? About 30 pounds." - Cindy Garner

"When women are depressed, they either eat or go shopping. Men invade another country. It's a whole different way of thinking." - Elaine Boosler

"I bought my wife a new car. She called and said, "There was water in the carburetor." I said, "Where's the car?" She said, "In the lake."" - Henny Youngman

"My mother buried three husbands, and two of them were just napping." - Rita Rudner

"People are always asking couples whose marriages have endured at least a quarter of a century for their secret for success. Actually, it is no secret at all. I am a forgiving woman. Long ago, I forgave my husband for not being Paul Newman." - Erma Bombeck

"A good rule of thumb is if you've made it to 35 and your job still requires you to wear a name tag, you've probably made a serious vocational error." -- Dennis Miller

"Anywhere is walking distance if you've got the time." -- Steven Wright

The Golf Drill

1. Back straight, knees bent, feet shoulder width apart.
2. Form a loose grip.
3. Keep your head down.
4. Avoid a quick back swing.
5. Stay out of the water.
6. Try not to hit anyone.
7. If you are taking too long, please let others go ahead of you.
8. Don't stand directly in front of others.
9. Quiet please ... while others are preparing to go.
10. Don't take extra strokes.
11. Very good. Now flush the urinal, wash your hands, go outside, and tee off.

Laws, of Sorts

Murphy's First Law for Wives: If you ask your husband to pick up five items at the store and then you add one more as an afterthought, he will forget two of the first five.

Kauffman's Paradox of the Corporation: The less important you are to the corporation, the more your tardiness or absence is noticed.

The Salary Axiom: The pay raise is just large enough to bump you into the next tax bracket and just small enough to have no effect on your take-home pay.

Miller's Law of Insurance: Insurance covers everything except what happens.

Weiner's Law of Libraries: There are no answers, only cross-references.

Isaac's Strange Rule of Staleness: Any food that starts out hard will soften when stale. Any food that starts out soft will harden when stale.

The Grocery Bag Law: The candy bar you planned to eat on the way home from the market is hidden at the bottom of the grocery bag.

Lampner's Law of Employment: When leaving work late, you will go unnoticed. When you leave work early, you will meet the boss in the parking lot.

More and More Lists

1. Save the whales. Collect the whole set.
2. A day without sunshine is like....night.
3. On the other hand....you have different fingers.
4. It's 99 % of lawyers give the rest a bad name.
5. Remember, half the people you know are below average.
6. He who laughs last, thinks slowest.
7. Depression is merely anger without enthusiasm.
8. Eagles may soar, but weasels don't get sucked into jet engines
9. The early bird may get the worm, but the second mouse gets the cheese.
10. I drive way too fast to worry about cholesterol.
11. I intend to live forever - so far, so good.
12. Borrow money from a pessimist - they don't expect it back.
13. Quantum mechanics: The dreams stuff is made of.
14. Support bacteria - they're the only culture some people have.
15. When everything's coming your way, you're in the wrong lane, and going the wrong way.
16. Experience is something you don't get until just after you need it.
17. Never do card tricks for the group you play poker with.
18. No one is listening until you make a mistake.
19. You never really learn to swear until you learn to drive.
20. The problem with the gene pool is that there is no lifeguard.
21. A clear conscience is usually the sign of a bad memory
22. Change is inevitable....except from vending machines.
23. Whoever believes in telekinesis raise my hand....
24. If at first you don't succeed, then skydiving isn't for you.

Ouch!

How do you catch a unique rabbit?
Unique up on it.

How do you catch a tame rabbit?
Tame way. Unique up on it.

How do crazy people go through the forest?
They take the psycho path.

How do you get holy water?
You boil the hell out of it.

What do fish say when they hit a concrete wall?

A Funny Thing Happened on the Way to the Health Fair

Dam!

What do Eskimos get from sitting on the ice too long?
Polaroid's

What do you call a boomerang that doesn't work?
A stick

What do you call cheese that isn't yours?
Nacho cheese

What Do You Call Santa's Helpers?
Subordinate Clauses.

What do you call four bullfighters in quicksand?
Quatro sinko.

What do you get from a pampered cow?
Spoiled milk.

What do you get when you cross a snowman with a vampire?
Frostbite.

What lies at the bottom of the ocean and twitches?
A nervous wreck.

What's the difference between roast beef and pea soup?
Anyone can roast beef.

Where do you find a dog with no legs?
Right where you left him.

Why do gorillas have big nostrils?
Because they have big fingers.

Why don't blind people like to sky dive?
Because it scares the dog.

What kind of coffee was served on the Titanic?
Sanka.

What Is the difference between a Harley and a Hoover?
The location of the dirt bag.

Why did pilgrims' pants always fall down?
Because they wore their belt buckle on their hat

What's the difference between a bad golfer and a bad skydiver?
A bad golfer goes, whack, dang! A bad skydiver goes dang! Whack.

What goes clop, clop, clop, bang, bang, clop, clop, clop?
An Amish drive-by shooting

How are a Texas tornado and a Tennessee divorce alike?
Somebody's gonna lose a trailer.

Definitions and Other Things

1. What's the definition of a teenager?
    God's punishment for enjoying sex.

2. Define Transvestite:
    A guy who likes to eat, drink and be Mary!

3. What's the difference between the Pope and your boss?
    The Pope only expects you to kiss his ring.

4. My mind works like lightning.
    One brilliant flash and it is gone.

5. The only time the world beats a path to your door is if you're in the bathroom.

6. I hate sex in the movies. Tried it once and the seat folded up.

7. It used to be only death and taxes were inevitable. Now, of course, there's shipping and handling, too.

8. A husband is someone who takes out the trash and gives the impression he just cleaned the whole house.

9. My next house will have no kitchen -- just vending machines.

10. The only thing wrong with a perfect drive to work is that you end up at work.

11. Americans are getting stronger. Twenty years ago, it took two people to carry ten dollars' worth of groceries. Today, a five-year-old can do it.

12. A blonde told her friend, "I was worried that my mechanic might try to

rip me off, so I was relieved when he told me all I needed was blinker fluid."

13. Why is a government worker like a shotgun with a broken firing pin? It won't work and you can't fire it.

14. I'm so depressed.. I went to the Doctor today and he refused to write me a prescription for Viagra. Said it would be like putting a new flagpole on a condemned building.

These are the 10 winners of the Bulwer-Lytton contest
wherein one writes only the first line of a bad novel.

10 - "As a scientist, Throckmorton knew that if he were ever to break wind in the echo chamber he would never hear the end of it."

9 - "Just beyond the Narrows the river widens."

8 - "With a curvaceous figure that Venus would have envied, a tanned, unblemished oval face framed with lustrous thick brown hair, deep azure-blue eyes fringed with long black lashes, perfect teeth that vied for competition, and a small straight nose, Marilee had a beauty that defied description."

7 - "Andre, a simple peasant, had only one thing on his mind as he crept along the east wall: "Andre creep... Andre creep... Andre creep."

6 - "Stanislaus Smedley, a man always on the cutting edge of narcissism, was about to give his body and soul to a back-alley sex-change surgeon to become the woman he loved."

5 - "Although Sarah had an abnormal fear of mice, it did not keep her from eking out a living at a local pet store."

4 - "Stanley looked quite bored and somewhat detached, but then penguins often do."

3 - "Like an overripe beefsteak tomato rimmed with cottage cheese, the corpulent remains of Santa Claus lay dead on the hotel floor."

2 - "Mike Hardware was the kind of private eye who didn't know the meaning of the word fear, a man who could laugh in the face of danger

and spit in the eye of death- in short, a moron with suicidal tendencies."

AND THE WINNER IS...

1 - "The sun oozed over the horizon, shoved aside darkness, crept along the greensward, and, with sickly fingers, pushed through the castle window, revealing the pillaged princess- hand at throat and crown asunder- gaping in frenzied horror at the sated, sodden amphibian lying beside her, screaming madly, "You lied!"

Something to Think About

If you throw a cat out the car window, does it become kitty litter?

If you choke a Smurf, what color does it turn?

What do you call a male ladybug?

What hair color do they put on the driver's license of a bald man?

When dog food is new and has an improved taste, who tests it?

Why didn't Noah swat those two mosquitoes?

Why do they sterilize the needle for lethal injections?

Why doesn't glue stick to the inside of the bottle?

Why do you need a driver's license to buy liquor when you can't drink and drive?

Why isn't phonetic spelled the way it sounds?

Why are there Interstate highways in Hawaii?

Why are there flotation devices in the seats of planes instead of parachutes?

Why are cigarettes sold at gas stations where smoking is prohibited?

If the 7-11 is open 24 hours a day, 365 days a year, why does it have locks on the door?

Why is a bra singular and panties plural?

How does the snowplow driver get to work?

If they squeeze olives to get olive oil, how do they get baby oil?

If a cow laughs, does milk come out of her nose?

Why don't sheep shrink when it rains?

If flying is so safe, why do they call the airport the terminal?

Democrat's Revenge - in Bumper Stickers

Don't Blame Me - I voted for Gore... I Think

UNPRESIDENTED!

If God Meant Us to Vote, He Would Have Given Us Candidates

What popular vote?

 I voted - Didn't matter

My parents retired to Florida and all I got was this lousy President

IT AIN'T OVER 'TIL YOUR BROTHER COUNTS THE VOTES

"Those who cast the votes decide nothing. Those who count the votes decide everything." --Joseph Stalin

Disney gave us Mickey, Florida gave us Dumbo

DON'T THROW AWAY YOUR VOTE... LET KATHERINE HARRIS DO IT FOR YOU

Who is this Chad guy and why is he pregnant.

Campaign spending: $184,000,000. Having your little brother rig the election for you: Priceless.

Bush trusts the people, but not if it involves counting.

Now do you understand the importance of user-testing?

To you I'm a drunk driver; to my friends, I'm presidential material!

One person, one vote (may not apply in certain states)

I DIDN'T VOTE FOR HIS DADDY EITHER

The election can't be broken. We just fixed it.

The skies (wheeze) of Texas (cough) are upon you! (choke)

Banana Republicans

George W. Bush: The President Quayle We Never Had

The last time somebody listened to a Bush, folks wandered in the desert for 40 years"

Facts of Life

1 - Raising teenagers is like nailing JELL-O to a tree.

2 - There is always a lot to be thankful for, if you take the time to look. For example, I'm sitting here thinking how nice it is that wrinkles don't hurt.

3 - The best way to keep kids at home is to make a pleasant atmosphere and let the air out of their tires.

4 - Families are like fudge . ... . mostly sweet, with a few nuts.
5 - Today's mighty oak is just yesterday's nut that held its ground.

Small Books

32. Al Gore: The Wild Years
31. Amelia Earhart's Guide to the Pacific Ocean
30. America's Most Popular Lawyers
29. Career Opportunities for Liberal Arts Majors
28. Detroit - A Travel Guide
27. Different Ways to Spell "Bob"

26. Dr. Kevorkian's Collection of Motivational Speeches
24. Ethiopian Tips on World Dominance
23. Everything Men Know About Women
22. Everything Women Know About Men
21. Famous Jewish Recipes for Pork
20. French Hospitality
19. George Foreman's Big Book of Baby Names
18. "How to Get to the Super Bowl" by Dan Marino
17. "How to Sustain a Musical Career" by Art Garfunkel
16. Human Rights Advances in China
15. "Life in a Quiet Neighborhood" by Elian Gonzales
14. Mike Tyson's Guide to Dating Etiquette
13. Mormon Recipes of Alcoholic Drinks
12. "My Plan To Find The Real Killers" by O J Simpson
11. "One Hundred and One Spotted Owl Recipes" by the EPA
09. Staple Your Way to Success
08. The Amish Phone Directory
07. The Engineer's Guide to Fashion
06. The Difference between Reality and Dilbert
05. "Things I can't afford" by Bill Gates
04. "Things I Wouldn't Do for Money" by Dennis Rodman
03. "Things I love about Bill" by Hillary Clinton
02. "To All The Men I've Loved Before" by Ellen DeGeneres

And the Number one World's Shortest book?
01. "The Book of Virtues and Morals" by Bill Clinton

Food for Thought

Last night I played a blank tape at full blast. The mime next door went nuts.

I went for a walk last night and my kids asked me how long I'd be gone. I said, "The whole time."

So what's the speed of dark?

How come you don't ever hear about gruntled employees?

Why don't they just make mouse-flavored cat food?

I just got skylights put in my place. The people who live above me are furious.

Isn't Disney World a people trap run by a mouse?

Whose cruel idea was it for the word "lisp" to have an "s" in it?

Light travels faster than sound. Is that why some people appear intelligent until you hear them speak?

How come "abbreviated" is such a long word?

Why do you press harder on a remote-control when you know the battery is dead?

Why are they called apartments, when they're all stuck together?

Why do banks charge you a "non-sufficient funds fee" when they already know you don't have any?

If the universe is everything, and scientists say that the universe is expanding, what is it expanding into?

If a tree falls in the forest and no one is around to see it, do the other trees make fun of it?

Why is a carrot more orange than an orange?

Why are there 5 syllables in the word "monosyllabic"?

Why do they call it the Department of Interior when they are in charge of everything outdoors?

Why is it, when a door is open it's ajar, but when a jar is open, it's not adore?

Tell a man that there are 400 billion stars and he'll believe you. Tell him a bench has wet paint and he has to touch it.

If Superman could stop bullets with his chest, why did he always duck when someone threw a gun at him?

Why does lemon juice contain "artificial ingredients" but dishwashing liquid contains "real lemons"?

Why do we wait until a pig is dead to "cure" it?

Why do we put suits in a garment bag and put garments in a suitcase?

Do Roman paramedics refer to IV's as "4's"?

What do little birdies see when they get knocked unconscious?

Why doesn't Tarzan have a beard?

Is boneless chicken considered an invertebrate?

I went to a bookstore and asked the saleswoman, "Where's the self-help section?" She said if she told me, it would defeat the purpose.

Isn't the best way to save face to keep the lower part shut?

Rules of Conduct

In General

1. Never take a beer to a job interview.

2. Always identify people in your yard before shooting at them.

3. It's considered tacky to take a cooler to church.

4. If you have to vacuum the bed, it is time to change the sheets.

5. Even if you're certain that you are included in the will, it is still considered tacky to drive a U-Haul to the funeral home.

Dining out

1. When decanting wine, make sure that you tilt the paper cup, and pour slowly so as not to "bruise" the fruit of the vine.

2. If drinking directly from the bottle, always hold it with your fingers covering the label.

Entertaining in Your Home

1. A centerpiece for the table should never be anything prepared by a taxidermist.

2. Do not allow the dog to eat at the table...no matter how good his or her

manners are.

Personal Hygiene

1. While ears need to be cleaned regularly, this is a job that should be done in private using one's *own* truck keys.

2. Proper use of toiletries can forestall bathing for several days. However, if you live alone, deodorant is a waste of good money.

3. Dirt and grease under the fingernails is a social no-no, as they tend to detract from a woman's jewelry and alter the taste of finger foods.

Dating (Outside the Family)

1. Always offer to bait your date's hook, especially on the first date.

2. Be aggressive. Let her know you're interested: "I've been wanting to go out with you since I read that stuff on the men's restroom wall two years ago."

3. Establish with her parents what time she is expected back. Some will say 10:00 PM; Others might say "Monday." If the latter is the answer, it is the man's responsibility to get her to school on time.

Theater Etiquette

1. Crying babies should be taken to the lobby and picked up immediately after the movie has ended.

2. Refrain from talking to characters on the screen. Tests have proven they can't hear you.

The Best Worst Country-Western Songs (Yep.... these are for real)

1. How Can I Miss You If You Won't Go Away?

2. You're the Reason Our Kids Are So Ugly
3. I've Been Flushed From The Bathroom Of Your Heart
4. I Keep Forgettin' I Forgot About You
5. She Got The Gold Mine and I Got The Shaft
6. My Wife Ran Off With My Best Friend And I Sure Do Miss Him
7. I Changed Her Oil, She Changed My Life
8. Drop-Kick Me Jesus Through The Goal Posts Of Life
9. Thank God And Greyhound She's Gone
10. If You Don't Leave Me Alone I'll Go And Find Someone Else Who Will
11. She Got The Ring And I Got The Finger
12. I've Got The Hungries For Your Love And I'm Waiting In Your Welfare Line
13. I Fell In A Pile Of You And Got Love All Over Me.
14. My John Deere Was Breaking Your Field While Your Dear John Was Breaking My Heart.
15. I Wouldn't Take Her To A Dawg Fight Because I'm Afraid She'd Win.
16. They May Put Me In Prison But They Can't Stop My Face From Breaking Out

The BIG Ifs

If you take an Oriental person and spin him around several times, does he become disoriented?

If people from Poland are called Poles, why aren't people from Holland called Holes?

If you mixed vodka and orange juice with milk of magnesia, would you get a Phillip's screwdriver?

If a pig loses it's voice, is it disgruntled?

If love is blind, why is lingerie so popular?

When someone asks you, "A penny for your thoughts" and you put your two cents in, what happens to the other penny?

Why is the man who invest all your money called a broker?

Why do croutons come in airtight packages? It's just stale bread to begin with.

When cheese gets its picture taken, what does it say?

Why is a person who plays the piano call a pianist, but a person who drives a race car not called a racist?

Why are a wise man and a wise guy opposite things?

If horrific means to make horrible, doesn't terrific mean to make terrible?

Why isn't 11 pronounced onety-one?

If lawyers are disbarred and clergymen are defrocked, doesn't it follow that electricians can be delighted, musicians denoted, cowboys deranged, models deposed, tree surgeons debarked and dry cleaners depressed?

From Your Friendly Neighborhood Phone Answering Machine

A is for academics, B is for beer. One of those reasons is why we're not here. So leave a message.

Hi. This is John. If you are the phone company, I already sent the money. If you are my parents, please send money. If you are my financial aid institution, you didn't lend me enough money. If you are my friends, you owe me money. If you are a female, don't worry, I have plenty of money.

Hi....... Now you say something.

Hi, I'm not home right now but my answering machine is, so you can talk to it instead. Wait for the beep.

Hello. I am David's answering machine. What are you?

Hello! This is Tom. If you leave a message, I will call you soon. If you leave a sexy message, I will call sooner!

Hi! John's answering machine is broken. This is his refrigerator. Please speak very slowly, and I'll stick your message to myself with one of these magnets.

Hello, this is Sally's microwave. Her answering machine just eloped with her tape deck, so I'm stuck with taking her calls. Say, if you want anything cooked while you leave your message, just hold it up to the phone.

Hello, you are talking to a machine. I am capable of receiving messages. My owners do not need new siding, new windows, or a hot tub, and their carpets are clean. They donate to charities through their office and do not need their picture taken. If you're still with me, leave your name and number and they will get back to you.

This is not an answering machine -- this is a telepathic thought-recording device. After the tone, think about your name, your reason for calling and a number where I can reach you, and I'll think about returning your call.

Hi! I am probably home. I'm just avoiding someone I don't like. Leave me a message, and if I don't call back, it's you.

Hi, this is George. I'm sorry I can't answer the phone right now. Leave a message, and then wait by your phone until I call you back.

If you are a burglar, then we're probably at home cleaning our weapons right now and can't come to the phone. Otherwise, we probably aren't home and it's safe to leave us a message.

You're growing tired. Your eyelids are getting heavy. You feel very sleepy now. You are gradually losing your willpower and your ability to resist suggestions. When you hear the tone you will feel helplessly compelled to leave your name, number, and a message.

Please leave a message. However, you have the right to remain silent. Everything you say will be recorded and will be used by us.

Hello, you've reached Jim and Sonya. We can't pick up the phone right now, because we're doing something we really enjoy. Sonya likes doing it up and down, and I like doing it left to right ... real slowly. So leave a message, and when we're done brushing our teeth, we'll get back to you.

Go, Gogh Team Go

After much careful research, it has been discovered that the artist Vincent Van Gogh had many relatives. Some them were:

His obnoxious brother	Please Gogh
His dizzy aunt	Verti Gogh
The brother who ate prunes	Gotta Gogh
The constipated uncle	Can't Gogh
The brother who worked at a convenience store	Stop'n Gogh
The grandfather from Yugoslavia	U Gogh

The brother who bleached his clothes white	Hue Gogh
The cousin from Illinois	Chica Gogh
His magician uncle	Wherediddy Gogh
His Italian uncle	Day Gogh
His Mexican cousin	Mee Gogh
The Mexican cousin's American half brother	Grin Gogh
The nephew who drove a stage coach	Wellsfar Gogh
The ballroom dancing aunt	Tan Gogh
A sister who loved disco	Go Gogh
The bird lover uncle	Flamin Gogh
His nephew psychoanalyst	E Gogh
The fruit loving cousin	Man Gogh
An aunt who taught positive thinking	Wayto Gogh
The little bouncy nephew	Poe Gogh
And his niece who travels the country in a van	Winnie Bay Gogh

.....and there we Gogh!

Mergermania

In the wake of the Exxon/Mobil deal and the AOL/Netscape deal, here are the following mergers we can expect to see:

1. Hale Business Systems, Mary Kay Cosmetics, Fuller Brush, & W.R. Grace. Company merge to become Hale Mary Fuller Grace.

2. Polygram Records, Warner Brothers, & Keebler Crackers will merge to become Polly-Warner-Cracker.

3. 3 M & Goodyear will merge to become MMMGood.

4. John Deere & Abitibi-Price will merge to become Deere Abi.

5. Zippo Manufacturing, Audi Motors, Dofasco, & Dakota Mining will merge to become Zip Audi Do Da.

6. Honeywell, Imasco, & Home Oil will merge to become Honey I'm Home.

7. Denison Mines, & Alliance & Metal Mining will merge to become Mine All Mine.

8. Federal Express & UPS will merge to become FED UPS

9. Xerox & Wurlitzer will merge and begin manufacturing reproductive organs.

10. Fairchild Electronics & Honeywell Computers will merge and become Fairwell Honeychild

11. 3 M, J.C. Penney & The Canadian Opera Company will merge and become 3 Penney Opera

12. Grey Poupon & Dockers Pants will merge and become Poupon Pants

13. Knott's Berry Farm & National Organization of Women will merge and become Knott NOW!

On & On

In case you needed further proof that the human race is doomed to stupidity, here are some actual label instructions on consumer goods:

On Sears hairdryer: *Do not use while sleeping.*
On a bag of Fritos: *You could be a winner! No purchase necessary. Details inside.*
On a bar of Dial soap: Directions: *Use like regular soap.*
On some Swann frozen dinners: *Serving suggestion: Defrost.*
On a hotel provided shower cap in a box: *Fits one head.*
On Tesco's Tiramisu dessert (printed on bottom of the box): *Do not turn upside down.*
On Marks & Spencer Bread Pudding: *Product will be hot after heating.*
On packaging for a Rowenta iron: *Do not iron clothes on body.*
On Boot's Children's cough medicine: *Do not drive car or operate machinery.*
On Nytol sleep aid: *Warning: May cause drowsiness.*
On a Korean kitchen knife: *Warning keep out of children.*
On a string of Chinese-made Christmas lights: *For indoor or outdoor use only.*
On a Japanese food processor: *Not to be used for the other use.*
On Sainsbury's peanuts: *Warning: contains nuts.*
On an American Airlines packet of nuts: *Instructions: open packet, eat nuts.*
On a Swedish chainsaw: *Do not attempt to stop chain with your hands or genitals.*
On a child's superman costume: *Wearing of this garment does not enable you to fly.*
On a box of crackers: *Do not eat package.*

ANAGRAM = rearranging letters into a phrase

Dormitory - When you rearrange the letters: Dirty Room

Evangelist - When you rearrange the letters: Evil's Agent

Desperation - When you rearrange the letters: A Rope Ends It
The Morse Code - When you rearrange the letters: Here Come Dots

Slot Machines -When you rearrange the letters: Cash Lost in 'em

Animosity - When you rearrange the letters: Is No Amity

Mother-in-law - When you rearrange the letters: Woman Hitler

Snooze Alarms - When you rearrange the letters: Alas! No More Z's

A Decimal Point - When you rearrange the letters: I'm a Dot in Place

The Earthquakes - When you rearrange the letters: That Queer Shake

Eleven plus Two - When you rearrange the letters: Twelve plus one

And for the grand finale!

PRESIDENT CLINTON OF THE USA
It can be rearranged (with no letters left over, and using each letter only once) into:
TO COPULATE HE FINDS INTERNS

Trailer Trash and Redneck sections pay homage to Jeff Foxworthy

You Know You're Trailer Trash When . . .

1. The Halloween pumpkin on your front porch has more teeth than your spouse.

2. You let your twelve-year-old daughter smoke at the dinner table in front of her kids.

3. You've been married three times and still have the same in-laws.

4. You think a woman who is "out of your league" bowls on a different night.

5. Jack Daniels makes your list of "Most Admired People."

6. You think Genitalia is an Italian airline.

7. You wonder how service stations keep their restrooms so clean.

8. Your Junior/Senior Prom had daycare.

9. You think the last words to The Star Spangled Banner are, "Gentlemen, start your engines."

10. The bluebook value of your truck goes up and down, depending on how much gas it has in it.

11. You have to go outside to get something out of the 'fridge.

12. You need one more hole punched in your card to get a freebie at the House of Tattoos.

13. You think loading the dishwasher means getting your wife drunk.

14. Your school fight song is "Dueling Banjos."

15. Your toilet paper has page numbers on it.

You Know You're a Redneck When...

You take your dog for a walk and you both use the same tree.
You can entertain yourself for more than an hour with a flyswatter.
Your property has been mistaken for a recycling center.
Your boat has not left the driveway in 15 years.
You burn your yard rather than mow it.
You think the Nutcracker is something you did off the high dive.
The Salvation Army declines your mattress.
Your entire family sat around waiting for a call from the governor to spare a loved one.
You offer to give someone the shirt off your back and they don't want it.

You have the local taxidermist on speed dial.
You come back from the dump with more than you took.
You keep a can of Raid on the kitchen table.
Your wife can climb a tree faster than your cat.
Your grandmother has "Ammo" on her Christmas list.
You've been kicked out of the zoo for heckling the monkeys.
The biggest city you've ever been to is Wal-Mart.
Your working TV sits on top of your non-working TV.
You thought the Unibomber was a wrestler.
You've used your ironing board as a buffet table.
You think a quarter horse is that ride in front of K-Mart.
Your neighbors think you're a detective because a cop always brings you home.
A tornado hits your neighborhood and does a $100,000 worth of improvement.
You've used a toilet brush as a back scratcher.
You missed 5th grade graduation because you had jury duty.
You think fast food is hitting a deer at 65 mph.
Somebody tells you that you've got something in your teeth and you take them out to see what it is.

From the Mouths of the Famous

"Ah, yes, divorce... from the Latin word meaning to rip out a man's genitals through his wallet."
-- Robin Williams

"Women complain about premenstrual syndrome, but I think of it as the only time of the month that I can be myself."
-- Roseanne

"Women need a reason to have sex. Men just need a place."
-- Billy Crystal

"You can say any foolish thing to a dog, and the dog will give you a look that says, 'My God, you're right! I never would've thought of that!'"
-- Dave Barry

"We have women in the military, but they don't put us in the front lines. They don't know if we can fight or if we can kill. I think we can. All the general has to do is walk over to the women and say, "You see the enemy over there? They say you look fat in those uniforms.' "
-- Elayne Boosler

"If you can't beat them, arrange to have them beaten."
-- George Carlin

"Instead of getting married again, I'm going to find a woman I don't like and just give her a house."
-- Lewis Grizzard

"The problem with the designated driver program, it's not a desirable job. But if you ever get sucked into doing it, have fun with it. At the end of the night, drop them off at the wrong house."
-- Jeff Foxworthy

"See, the problem is that God gives men a brain and a penis, and only enough blood to run one at a time."
-- Robin Williams

If a woman has to choose between catching a fly ball and saving an infant's life, she will choose to save the infant's life without even considering if there is a man on base.
-- Dave Barry

What do people mean when they say the computer went down on them?
-- Marilyn Pittman

Relationships are hard. It's like a full time job, and we should treat it like one. If your boyfriend or girlfriend wants to leave you, they should give you two weeks' notice. There should be severance
pay, and before they leave you, they should have to find you a temp.
-- Bob Ettinger

My mom said she learned how to swim when someone took her out in the lake and threw her off the boat. I said, 'Mom, they weren't trying to teach you how to swim...'"
-- Paula Poundstone

A study in the Washington Post says that women have better verbal skills than men. I just want to say to the authors of that study:.......Duh.
-- Conan O'Brien

Why does Sea World have a seafood restaurant?? I'm halfway through my fish burger and I realize, Oh my God....I could be eating a slow learner.
-- Lynda Montgomery

I think that's how Chicago got started. A bunch of people in New York said, "Gee, I'm enjoying the crime and the poverty, but it just isn't cold enough. Let's go west."

-- Richard Jeni

If life was fair, Elvis would be alive and all the impersonators would be dead.
-- Johnny Carson

Sometimes I think war is God's way of teaching us geography.
-- Paul Rodriguez

In elementary school, in case of fire you have to line up quietly in a single file line from smallest to tallest. What is the logic? Do tall people burn slower?
-- Warren Hutcherson

"I worry that the person who thought up Muzak may be thinking up something else."
-- Lily Tomlin

Some women hold up dresses that are so ugly and they always say the same thing: "This looks much better on...." On what? On fire?
-- Marsha Warfield

Bigamy is having one wife too many. Monogamy is the same.
-- Oscar Wilde

Suppose you were an idiot... And suppose you were a member of Congress.... But I repeat myself.
-- Mark Twain

Our bombs are smarter than the average high school student. At least they can find Kuwait.
-- A. Whitney Brown

Section Sixteen: Round Pegs, Square Holes

This Chapter is about all those stories that don't seem to fit any particular category.
This explanation is designed to save you from trying to figure it out.

Beethoven's Requiem

When Beethoven passed away, he was buried in a churchyard. A couple days later, the town drunk was walking through the cemetery and heard some strange noise coming from the area where Beethoven was buried. Terrified, the drunk ran and got the priest to come and listen to it. The priest bent close to the grave and heard some faint, unrecognizable music coming from the grave.

Frightened, the priest ran and got the town magistrate.

When the magistrate arrived, he bent his ear to the grave, listened for a moment, and said, "Ah, yes, that's Beethoven's Ninth Symphony, being played backwards."

He listened a while longer, and said, "There's the Eight Symphony, and it's backwards, too. Most puzzling." The magistrate kept listening for hours, "There's the Seventh... the Sixth... the Fifth..."

Suddenly the realization of what was happening dawned on the magistrate. He stood up and announced to the crowd that had gathered in the cemetery, "My fellow citizens, there's nothing to worry about. It's just Beethoven decomposing."

Claude, the Magnificent

It was opening night at the Orpheum and the Claude, the Magnificent, was topping the bill. Hundreds of people came from miles around to see the famed hypnotist do his stuff. As Claude took to the stage, he announced, "unlike most stage hypnotists who invite two or three people up onto the stage to be put into a trance, I intend to hypnotize each and every member of this audience."

The excitement was almost electric as Claude withdrew a beautiful antique pocket watch from his coat and said, "I want you each to keep your eyes on this antique pocket watch. It's a very special watch. It's been in my family for six generations.

He began to swing the watch gently back and forth while chanting, "Watch the watch, watch the watch, watch the watch ..." The crowd became mesmerized as the watch swung back and forth, light gleaming off its polished surface.

Hundreds of pairs of eyes followed the swinging watch, until suddenly it slipped from the hypnotist's fingers and fell to the floor breaking into a hundred pieces.

"Shit," said the hypnotist.

It took three weeks to clean up the theater.

Dental Disaster

A man went to his dentist because he feels something wrong in his mouth. The dentist examined him and said, "That new upper plate I put in for you six months ago is eroding. What have you been eating?"

The man replied, "All I can think of is that about four months ago my wife made some asparagus and put some stuff on it that was delicious - Hollandaise sauce, she called it. I loved it so much I now put it on everything- meat, toast, fish, vegetables, everything."

"Well," said the dentist, "That's probably the problem. Hollandaise sauce is made with lots of lemon juice, which is highly corrosive. It's eaten away part of your upper plate.

I'll make you a new plate, and this time use chrome."

"Why chrome?" asked the patient.

To which the dentist replied, "It's simple. Everyone knows that there's no plate like chrome for the Hollandaise!"

Ah, Watson!

Sherlock Holmes and Dr. Watson go on a camping trip, set up their tent, talk for awhile and fall asleep. Some hours later, Holmes wakes his faithful friend. "Watson, look up at the sky and tell me what you see."

Watson replies, "I see millions of stars."

"What does that tell you?"

Watson ponders for a minute. "Astronomically speaking, it tells me that there are millions of galaxies and potentially billions of planets.

Astrologically, it tells me that Saturn is in Leo. Time wise, it appears to be approximately a quarter past three. Theologically, it's evident the Lord is all-powerful and we are small and insignificant. Meteorologically, it seems we will have a beautiful day tomorrow. What does it tell you?"

Holmes is silent for a moment, then speaks. "Watson, you idiot! Someone has stolen our tent!!!"

The Ostrich

A man walks into a restaurant with an ostrich behind him, and as he sits, the waitress comes over and asks for their order. The man says,"I'll have a hamburger, fries and a coke." The waitress turns to the ostrich. "What's yours?" "I'll have the same,"says the ostrich.

The waitress returns with the order. The man asks "How much is this?"

"That will be $18.40 please," she responds. The man reaches into his pocket and pulls out the exact change for payment.

The next day, the man and the ostrich come again. The man orders the same thing, a hamburger, fries and a coke." The ostrich says, "I'll have the same." Once again the man reaches into his pocket and pays with exact change.

This becomes a routine until late one evening, the two enter again. "The usual?" asks the waitress. "No, this is Saturday night. I'll have a steak, baked potato, onion rings and a salad," says the man. "Same for me," says the ostrich. The waitress bring the order and leaves the check for $32.58. Once again the man pulls exact change out of his pocket and places it on the table.

The waitress can't hold back her curiosity any longer. "Excuse me, sir. How do you manage to always come up with the exact change out of your pocket every time?"

"Well," says the man, "several years ago I was cleaning the attic and I found an old lamp. When I rubbed it a Genie appeared and offered me two wishes. My first wish was that if I ever had to pay for anything, I just put my hand in my pocket, and the right amount of money would always be there."

"That's brilliant!" says the waitress. "Most people would wish for a million dollars or something, but you'll always be as rich as you want for as long as you live!" "Whether it's a gallon of milk or a Rolls Royce, the exact money is always there," says the man.

The waitress asks, "One other thing, sir, what's with the ostrich?"

The man replies, a little sadly and with a sigh, "My second wish was for a chick with long legs."

Not Exactly the Sistine Chapel

There was a Scottish tradesman, a painter called Jock, who was very interested in making a dollar where he could. He often would thin down his paint to make it go a wee bit further.

As it happened, he got away with this for some time, but eventually the Presbyterian Church decided to do a big restoration job on the roof of one of their biggest churches. Jock put in a bid and because his price was so low, he got the job.

He put the scaffolding, bought the paint and ... yes, I am sorry to say, thinning it down with the turpentine.

Jock was up on the scaffolding, painting away, the job nearly done, when suddenly there was a horrendous clap of thunder, and the sky opened and the rain poured down, washing the thin paint from all over the church. Jock was knocked off the scaffold and landed on the lawn, among the gravestones, surrounded by telltale puddles of the thinned and useless paint.

Jock was no fool. He knew this was a judgment from the Almighty, so he fell on his knees and cried: "Oh, God! Forgive me! What should I do?"

And from the thunder, a mighty Voice spoke: "Repaint! Repaint and thin no more!"

Yes, Virginia, There is a Santa....But Not This One

'Twas the night before Christmas -
Old Santa was pissed
He cussed out the elves and threw down his list

Miserable little brats, ungrateful little jerks
I have good mind to scrap the whole works

I've busted my ASS for damn near a year
Instead of "Thanks, Santa" - what do I hear

The old lady bitches cause I work late at night
The elves want more money - The reindeer all fight

Rudolph got drunk and goosed all the maids
Donner is pregnant and Vixen has AIDS

And just when I thought that things would get better
Those ass holes from IRS sent me a letter

They say I owe taxes - if that ain't damn funny
Who the hell ever sent Santa Clause any money

And the kids these days - they all are the pits
They want the impossible ...Those mean little shits

I spent a whole year making wagons and sleds
Assembling dolls...Their arms, legs and heads

I made a ton of yo-yo's - No request for them
They want computers and robots...they think I'm IBM!

Flying through the air...dodging the trees
Falling down chimneys and skinning my knees

I'm quitting this job...there's just no enjoyment
I'll sit on my fat ass and draw unemployment

There's no Christmas this year...
Now you know the reason -
I found me a blonde.
I'm going SOUTH for the season!!

Music to My Ears

There was this guy who had a girlfriend named Lorraine who was very
pretty and he liked her a lot. One day he went to work and found that a
new girl had started working there. Her name was Clearly and she was

absolutely gorgeous.

He became quite besotted with Clearly and after a while it became obvious that she was interested in him too. But this guy was a loyal man and he wouldn't do anything with Clearly while he was still going out with Lorraine. He decided that time had come to break up with Lorraine and start dating Clearly. He planned several times to tell Lorraine but he couldn't bring himself to do it.

One day they went for a walk along the riverbank when Lorraine slipped and fell into the river. The current carried her off and she drowned. The guy stopped for a moment by the river and then ran off smiling and singing...

Now it gets really bad...

"I can see Clearly now Lorraine has gone!!!

I was Wondering?

Miller was a moderately successful stockbroker who dreamed of making the big money someday. He took his friend out for a drive, and he chose the route carefully in order to impress on him the possibilities of the brokerage business.

"Look at that yacht," he said as they drove slowly past a marina. "That belongs to the senior partner at Merrill Lynch. That one over there is owned by the head of Goldman, Sachs. And look at that huge yacht out there. That's the pride and joy of the top seller at Prudential-Bache."

His friend was silent. Miller turned to look at him and saw a pained look on his face. "What's the matter?" Miller asked.

"I was just wondering," his friend said. "Are there any customers' yachts?"

Job Appreciation

When you have an "I hate my job" day, try this: On your way home from work, stop at your local pharmacy and go to the thermometer section. You will need to purchase a rectal thermometer made by "Q-tip." Be very sure that you get this brand. When you get home, lock your doors, draw the drapes, and disconnect the phone so that you will not be disturbed during your therapy.

Change your clothing to something very comfortable, such as a sweat suit and lie down on your bed. Open the package and remove the thermometer. Carefully place it on the bedside table so that it will not become chipped or broken. Take out the written material that accompanies the thermometer and read it. You will notice that in small print there is a statement: "Every rectal thermometer made by Q-tip is personally tested."

Now, close your eyes and repeat out loud five times, "I am so glad I do not work in quality control at the Q-tip Company."

The Question

A young boy went up to his father and asked him, "Dad, what is the difference between potentially and realistically?"

The father thought for a moment, then answered, "Go ask your mother if she would sleep with Tony Bennett for a million dollars. Then ask your sister if she would sleep with Tom Cruise for a million dollars, and ask your brother if he'd sleep with Tom Cruise for a million dollars. Come back and tell me what you learn from that."

So the boy went to his mother and asked, "Would you sleep with Tony Bennett for a million dollars?"

The mother replied, "Of course I would! I wouldn't pass up an opportunity like that."

The boy then went to his sister and asked, "Would you sleep Tom Cruise for a million dollars?"

The girl replied, "Oh my God! I would just love to do that! I would be nuts to pass up that opportunity!"

The boy then went to his brother and asked, "Would you sleep with Tom Cruise for a million dollars?"

"Of course," the brother replied. "Do you know how much a million could buy?"

The boy pondered that for a few days, then went back to his dad.

His father asked him, "Did you find out the difference between potentially and realistically?"

The boy replied, "Yes, sir. Potentially, we're sitting on three million dollars, but realistically, we're living with two sluts and a fag."

The Numbers Game

Ever wonder about those people who say they are giving more than 100%?

We have all been to those meetings where someone wants over 100%.

How about achieving 103%? Here's a little math that might prove helpful.

What makes life 100%?

If A B C D E F G H I J K L M N O P Q R S T U V W X Y Z are represented as:
1 2 3 4 5 6 7 8 9 10 11 12 13 14 15 16 17 18 19 20 21 22 23 24 25 26

Then
H A R D W O R K
8 1 18 4 23 15 18 11 = 98%

K N O W L E D G E
11 14 15 23 12 5 4 7 5 = 96%

But
A T T I T U D E
1 20 20 9 20 21 4 5 = 100%

And
B U L L S H I T
2 21 12 12 19 8 9 20 = 103%

So, it stands to reason that hard work and knowledge will get you close, **attitude** will get you there, but **bullshit** will put you over the top.

Oh, Hell

The following is an actual question given on a University of Washington engineering mid-term. The answer was so "profound" that the Professor shared it with colleagues.

Bonus Question: Is Hell exothermic (gives off heat) or endothermic (absorbs heat)? Most of the students wrote proofs of their beliefs using Boyle's Law, (gas cools off when it expands and heats up when it is compressed) or some variant. One student, however, wrote the following:

"First, we need to know how the mass of Hell is changing in time. So we need to know the rate that souls are moving into Hell and the rate they are leaving. I think that we can safely assume that once a soul gets to Hell, it will not leave. Therefore, no souls are leaving.

As for how many souls are entering Hell, lets look at the different religions that exist in the world today. Some of these religions state that if you are not a member of their religion, you will go to Hell. Since there are more than one of these religions and since people do not Belong to more than one religion, we can project that all souls go to Hell. With birth and death rates as they are, we can expect the number of souls in Hell to increase exponentially.

Now, we look at the rate of change of the volume in Hell because Boyle's Law states that in order for the temperature and pressure in Hell to stay the same, the volume of Hell has to expand as souls are added.

This gives two possibilities:

1. If Hell is expanding at a slower rate than the rate at which souls enter Hell, then the temperature and pressure in Hell will increase until all Hell breaks loose.

2. Of course, if Hell is expanding at a rate faster than the increase of souls in Hell, then the temperature and pressure will drop until Hell freezes over. So which is it?

If we accept the postulate given to me by Ms. Teresa Banyan during my freshman year, "...that it will be a cold day in Hell before I sleep with you," and take into account the fact that I still have not succeeded in having sexual relations with her, then, #2 cannot be true, and thus I am sure that Hell is exothermic and will not freeze."

The student received the only "A" given.

Dumb is as Dumb Does

A Help Desk employee was fired; however, he/she is currently suing the

A Funny Thing Happened on the Way to the Health Fair

Word Perfect organization for "Termination without Cause."

Actual recorded dialogue of a former WordPerfect Customer Support employee:

"Ridge Hall, computer assistance; may I help you?" *"Yes, well, I'm having trouble with WordPerfect."*

"What sort of trouble?" *"Well, I was just typing along, and all of a sudden the words went away."*

"Went away?" *"They disappeared."*

"Hmm. So what does your screen look like now?" *"Nothing."*

"Nothing?" *"It's blank; it won't accept anything when I type."*

"Are you still in WordPerfect, or did you get out?? *"How do I tell?"*

"Can you see the C: prompt on the screen?" *"What's a sea-prompt?"*

"Never mind, can you move your cursor around the screen?" *"There isn't any cursor. I told you, it won't accept anything I type."*

"Does your monitor have a power indicator?" *"What's a monitor?*

"It's the thing with the screen on it that looks like a TV. Does it have a little light that tells you when it's on?" *"I don't know."*

"Well, then look on the back of the monitor and find where the power cord goes into it. Can you see that?" *"Yes, I think so."*

"Great, follow the cord to the plug, and tell me if it's plugged into the wall." *"Yes, it is."*

"When you were behind the monitor, did you notice that there were two cables plugged into the back of it, not just one?" *"No."*

"Well, there are. I need you to look back there again and find the other cable." *"Okay, here it is."*

"Follow it for me, and tell me if it's plugged securely into the back of your computer." *"I can't reach."*

"Uh huh. Well, can you see if it is?" *"No."*

"Even if you maybe put your knee on something and lean way over?" *"Oh, it's not because I don't have the right angle - it's because it's dark."*

"Dark?" *"Yes - the office light is off, and the only light I have is coming in from the window."*

"Well, turn on the office light then." *"I can't."*

"No? Why not?" *"Because there's a power failure."*

"A power... a power failure? Aha, Okay, we've got it licked now. Do you still have the boxes and manuals and packing stuff your computer came in?" *"Well, yes, I keep them in the closet."*

"Good. Go get them, and unplug your system and pack it up just like it was when you got it. Then take it back to the store you bought it from." *"Really? Is it that bad?"*

"Yes, I'm afraid it is." *"Well, all right then, I suppose. What do I tell them?"*

"Tell them you're too stupid to own a computer."

May your laughter never end...but this book has!

God Bless, America!

About the Editor

Fred Neil was an award winning News and Sports Director for the Metromedia radio station, WCBM, Baltimore and produced the Baltimore Colt Football play-by-play broadcasts, produced, wrote, and co-hosted series with such sports luminaries as Johnny Unitas, Jimmy Orr, Ordell Braase, and Tom Matte of the Colts and Brooks Robinson of the Baltimore Orioles.

Neil served as Press Officer for Mayor of Baltimore, William Donald Schaefer,who was later elected Governor of Maryland. He has also served as president of the Maryland Press Club, Baltimore Press and Sports Reports Associations.

He co-authored, the very funny sports biography "It's a Very Simple Game! The Life and Times and Charley Eckman." The book, published in 1995, has a foreword by Tom Clancy and received rave reviews from such sports notables as Dean Smith, legendary former coach of the University of North Carolina; Larry Brown, NBA Basketball Coach; Billy Packer, CBS Basketball analyst; Frank DeFord, nationally acclaimed sports writer; Boog Powell, Oriole great and Art Donovan, Pro Football Hall of Famer.

Married to the former Dawn Fischer, he has three children from a previous marriage, Jay, Brian and Gail.

Printed in the United States
5496